A *lost* Sheep of Shenandoah

Charles Edwin Rinker of Virginia
and Harry Bernard King of Iowa:
DNA Reveals
They Were the Same Man

The Rev Dr. Cynthia Vold Forde

Editor Ronald S. Beatty

authorHOUSE®

AuthorHouse™
1663 Liberty Drive
Bloomington, IN 47403
www.authorhouse.com
Phone: 833-262-8899

Published by AuthorHouse 05/12/2022

ISBN: 978-1-6655-5575-3 (sc)
ISBN: 978-1-6655-5574-6 (e)

Library of Congress Control Number: 2022905625

Cover photo provided by Cottonbro through pexels.com
Cover Graphics: Peter Grossman

Print information available on the last page.

Artwork by 7 year old Fyn Rose Forde, by
Charlie's 13th great granddaughter.

Dedicated to my beloved aunts

Betty Miller Francis and JoAnn Miller Eid without whose DNA this book never would have been written.

With Gratitude

Deepest thanks to aunts Betty Miller Francis, and JoAnn Eid who lived long enough to learn the truth about their grandfather, and to my cousins, Carol, Margie, Beverly, Terry and David, I love you! A special thanks to my husband, editor, and computer geek, Ron Beatty, who never complains or grumbles about helping me. A special thanks to my newly discovered and beloved Youmans and Rinker cousins, Kathy, and Barbara, for participating in this amazing discovery; our universe is expanding with love for each other.

Participants have given the author written permissions to use their names and publish this research.

Contents

Testimonials

"Ancestors sometimes appear in a location as if deposited there out of the blue. Harry Bernard King was one of those until DNA revealed two names, four families, and his origins a thousand miles away." A Lost Sheep of Shenandoah

"Discovering her grandfather was an imposter was a shock and disappointment for Betty Miller Francis; It was bizarre! We experienced betrayal and disbelief. Yet, I am so grateful, Cynthia, for your perseverance in seeking the truth for the sake of the family." Carol Francis Rinehart

"My first thoughts were it's amazing you figured this out! Given only female offspring survived that generation, it might be useful to have some offspring that carried the male DNA. Also, it must have been more common occurrence than we thought in those days and is a part of many family stories. We are so blessed with all the incredible information and stories you have developed and shared with the descendants. It helps us understand our ancestral past, the bad and the good and how we've progressed to the present day. I always announce with pride that we are descendants. Thanks, Cynthia!!" Beverly Odom

"The discovery of the lost sheep, "Charles Edwin Rinker", had my mother's curiosity. She knew her Grandfather as Harry King. Jo Ann Miller Eid would have loved to have read this final story. Her first thought was sadness as she wished she could have met his other families. Thanks for bringing our history to light." Terry Eid Harris

"Thank you so much, Cousin Cynthia, for all of your hard work and dedication that has gone into publishing this book. You have unlocked a mystery that has brought the Rinker family into a new sense of belonging. For that I am truly grateful. This is a wonderful blessing." Barbara Rinker Fann

Foreword

from Pastor & Author, Kathy A. Weckwerth
(Great-granddaughter of Charles Rinker).

There is no greater inward desire than to know where one has come from. We all have some innate longing to discover our starting point. A reason. A purpose. A connection. We want to know who we are becoming, and how we managed to arrive here.

It's not just a desire to know that we were created from the hand of Almighty God, but a desire to understand a connection from our own delicate strands of genetic DNA. Who were our relatives? What made them strong? What made them unique in this big story of history?

As I set out on a path to discover the truth of who my great-grandfather was, never in my wildest dreams would I believe it would have lead me to the Rev. Dr. Cynthia Forde-Beatty. And yet it did. Not only did it lead me to her, but it led me to find out just how perfectly she fit into my own unique heritage. Without her efforts and research, I fear I would still be in the dark about my family lineage.

In this book, Dr. Rev. Cynthia used her brilliant mind, research skills, shepherd's heart, and tenacious attitude, to research our family's history. Her discovery led us to the certainty and understanding of our past. I was humbled to find Cynthia, a knowledgeable genealogist, as an intricate part of my family tree.

As you begin to read through the pieces of the woven fabrics of our family's history, you will find fascinating truths within her detailed and documented events and records.

Each step that Cynthia took, led the two of us closer to finding each other, and brought us closer to that ultimate discovery of our past. A mysterious shared biological great-grandfather, with a tumultuous life, now unites us forever as family.

Cynthia's book about our great-grandfather, Charles Rinker, will lead you from beginning to end on a surprising journey of intrigue, desertion, and secrecy.

Over these past few years, I have sat on the sidelines and watched her as she worked diligently for hours upon hours, researching this life-changing discovery.

Desperate and searching for answers to my past, Cynthia led me from an old cement headstone deep within the grounds of an Iowa graveyard, to an insightful revelation of my family tree. She revealed the pieces of our family's lives and how they gracefully and perfectly connected throughout time.

I will forever be grateful to Dr. Rev. Cynthia for her discovery, for in that knowledge and revelation, I am finally at peace with who I am and where I have come from. Not a perfect family. Not a perfect past. But one that has led us to where we are, and who we are becoming. And for that, I now revel in truth, knowledge … and freedom from the unknown.

Preface

About the author: *Cynthia became interested in genealogy and pursued her ancestry with vigor but was stymied by one great-grandfather, Harry Bernard King, who arrived in Worth County, Iowa in 1894, who was born on 17 Dec 1866 near Mt. Solon, Virginia, whose obituary asserts that his mother died when he was four and his father died when he was fourteen. For thirty plus years, Cynthia analyzed census records every imaginable way, hired professionals to hunt for Mr. King several times, and spent a bundle researching with traditional genealogy trying to authenticate him in Virginia.* Ronald S. Beatty, Editor

My great-grandfather was Harry Bernard King who moved to Worth County, Iowa in 1894, from Virginia, according to his obituary written by his oldest daughter, Ruby Anna King Miller, his marriage application, and census records.

Thirty-five years of research by eight outstanding professional genealogists added nothing to the earlier life story of Harry Bernard King. No connection to Virginia could be found for Harry, who became my great-grandfather. The compelling question remained, "Why would a 28-year-old young man move from the beautiful Blue Ridge Mountains of Virginia to the flat fields of Worth County, Iowa in 1894?" In 2017, DNA solved this mystery of a man who could change his identity but not his DNA.

The Kings had four daughters but no son, hence, no Y-DNA. Only one daughter had biological children. In 2011, my two aunts, his granddaughters, participated in atDNA (autosomal) testing at Family Tree DNA. Imagine our surprise to discover a very close cousin match to a male descendant of Harry King's 19-year-old neighbor, Emma Youmans; she may not have realized she was pregnant until after Harry had married my great-grandmother, Anna Schulz. The Youmans male had participated in atDNA testing to learn the paternity of his ancestor. Because there were no other possibilities, we were certain, "We now have Harry King's Y-DNA, and tested at FamilyTreedna.com," This was to no avail –we had no more matches.[1]

Six years later in March 2017, we were again surprised by a very close similar match on GEDmatch.com to a great granddaughter of a man with the exact birthdate of Harry King. Charles Edwin Rinker was born in Ashby, Shenandoah County, Virginia on December 17, 1866; his mother died when he was four, and his father died when he was sixteen, nearly identical to the ages given in Harry King's obituary. Charles Rinker's grandmother was Anna Kingree Moore whereas Harry King had stated that his mother was Anna Moore.[2] Charlie had married, but he abandoned his wife, Catherine.[3]

---

[1] "Family Finder," *FamilyTreeDNA* (www.FTDNA.com: 23 Aug 2013), "Matches" with Aunt Betty shows Aunt Jo and reveals Dave; results from this dynamic database require a private passcode and kit number; correspondence with Dave

[2] "One to Many," *GEDmatch* (www.GEDMatch.com: Ver: Mar 27 2017 18:41:59) with Aunt Betty shows Aunt Jo and Dave and reveals X correspondence with Connie's Family Tree," *Ancestry* (www.Ancestry.com: accessed 27 Mar 2017), Charles Edwin Rinker

[3] "Family Tree," *Ancestry* (www.Ancestry.com: accessed 27 Mar 2017), Charles Edwin Rinker; United States Federal Census records of Shenandoah County, Virginia, *Ancestry* (www.Ancestry.com), see individual citations in Charles Rinker Timeline below; e-mail correspondence.

Yet another surprise awaited with the discovery of Charlie's second marriage in Indiana; a Charles E. Rinker married Alma Blanche Krou on 18 September 1892 in St. Joseph, Indiana, she was a daughter of Jacob Krou and Ruth Moon; this Charles E. Rinker was also born 17 December 1866 in Ashby, Shenandoah County, Virginia. Steve Krou, a Krou family historian, notes: *"Shortly before the birth of their son Frederick, his first and legal wife from Virginia showed up with three children back in Virginia, Charles took off never to be heard from again."* An 80-year-old grandson of Charles and Alma's is elated to learn about his grandfather and participated in Y-DNA testing to provide conclusive evidence that Charles Edwin Rinker, Charles E. Rinker and Harry Bernard King were indeed one and the same man.[4]

And that is exactly why a young man from Virginia moved to Worth County, Iowa in 1894 and changed his name, but he could not change his DNA.

---

[4] "Indiana, Marriage Index, 1800-1941," *Ancestry* (www.Ancestry.com: 2005), marriage, Indiana, Charles E. Rinker; citing Works Progress Administration, comp., Index to Marriage Records, Indiana; *Ancestry* search for Alma Krau discovered *Find-A-Grave* (www.findagrave.com: 13 Mar 2017); e-mail correspondence 13 Mar 2017 with Steve Krou and others; "Zanabeth1 Family Tree," *Ancestry* (www.ancestry.com: 13 Mar 2017), Charles E. Rinker; discovered Bob

Ancestors sometimes appear in a location as if deposited there out of the blue. Harry Bernard King was one of those until DNA revealed two names, four families, and his origins a thousand miles away.

Harry Bernard King, about 28 years old, appeared in Worth County, Iowa, in 1894. He married there in 1896 and had five children.[5] His 1919 obituary said he was born and raised in Virginia, but no documentary evidence could be found for him in that state.[6] Autosomal and Y-DNA linked Harry to his Virginia origins under another name, revealing two additional marriages and an illegitimate son.

---

[5] *1910*; *Grove, Worth, Iowa*; Roll: *T624_429*; Page: *4A*; Enumeration District: *0172*; FHL microfilm: *1374442*

[6] The author would like to thank the following genealogists for assisting in her attempt to find a documentary record for Harry in Virginia over a period of thirty-five years: George Ott, Raquel Lindaas, Jane E. Sherman, Ronald S. Beatty, and Barbara Vines Little. For details of negative searches, see client reports by these genealogists, personally held by the author. Links were checked 8 and 9 February 2021. Participants written permissions to publish the research are in the possession of the author.

Harry Bernard King, of Iowa

17 December 1866
Mt. Solon, Augusta, Virginia

H. B. King, 31, and Anna Schulz, 19, were married in Charles City, Floyd County, Iowa, on 28 December 1896 by C. D. Merriam, Justice of the Peace. The marriage took place twenty miles from the home of Anna's grandfather, Peter E. Wagner, at Osage, Mitchell County, Iowa.[7] Likely the couple eloped, as no family or friends witnessed the marriage. H. Morgan Davis, a resident of Osage, provided a

---

[7] Anna's mother, Barbara Schultz, was a daughter of Peter Wagner as shown by her death record and several census records. "Iowa, U.S., Death Records, 1920–1967, imaged at *Ancestry* (https://www.ancestry.com/imageviewer/collections/61442/images/101784610 00426), Worth County, Mrs. Barbara Wagner Schultz, 13 May 1925. Also, 1870 U.S. census, Dane County, Wisconsin, population schedule, Springfield, page 27, dwelling 170, family 170, Peter Wagner; imaged at *Ancestry* (https://www.ancestry.com/imageviewer/collections/7163/images/4268454 00416). Also, 1880 U.S. census, Mitchell County, Iowa, population schedule, Osage Township, Enumeration District (ED) 309, page 10-B, dwelling 91, family 94, Peter E. Wagner; imaged at *Ancestry* (https://www.ancestry.com/imageviewer/collections/6742/images/4240928-00529). Also, 1885 Iowa census, Mitchell County, Cedar Township, page 50, dwelling 66, family 1, Peter Wagner; imaged at *Ancestry* (https://www.ancestry.com/imageviewer/collections/1084/images/IA1885_234-0043).

notarized statement attesting to the age and marital status of both bride and groom.[8]

According to the marriage application, the bride was of Kensett, Iowa, and a daughter of Carl and Barbara Schulz.[9] Anna was born on 28 February 1877 in Waunakee, Dane County, Wisconsin.[10] The marriage record added that H. B. King was born in Mt. Solon, Augusta County, Virginia, to John King and Anna Moore.[11]

---

[8] Floyd County, Iowa, Marriage Record "G", Page 536; Marriage Register & Index 1896-1900, Page 139

[9] Floyd County, Iowa, Marriage Record "G", Page 536; Marriage Register & Index 1896-1900, page 139

[10] 1880 U.S. census, Dane County, Wisconsin, population schedule, Springfield Town, Enumeration District (ED) 89, page 23, dwelling 181, family 189, Carl Schulz; imaged at Ancestry (https://www.ancestry.com/imageviewer/collections/6742/images/4244707-00344). Also, 1895 Iowa census, Worth County, Kensett Township, page 11, dwelling 51, family 52, Carl Schultz; imaged at *Ancestry* (https://www.ancestry.com/imageviewer/collections/1084/images/IA1885_416-0217).
Also, Anna Schultz King Painter memorial: *Find-A-Grave* (https://www.findagrave.com/memorial/80960536: accessed July 2020), memorial for Anna Shultz Painter, (28 February 1877-19 April 1941), Sunset Rest Cemetery, Northwood, Worth County, Iowa.

[11] "Iowa, U.S., Marriage Records, 1880–1951," Floyd County, King-Schultz, 26 December 1896; imaged at *Ancestry* (https://www.ancestry.com/imageviewer/collections/8823/images/42563_fp030872_0093-00211).

Harry and Anna lived in Kensett, Worth County, Iowa until 1910, after which they moved to Grove Township, Northwood County, Iowa.[12] Harry died at age 52 from complications of diabetes.[13]

Harry's obituaries provided an outline of his life[14]:

- Born 17 December 1866 in Stanton, Augusta County, Virginia
- Lost his mother when he was four and his father, a Confederate veteran, when he was 14
- Came to Iowa from Virginia at age 28, which would be 1894
- Married Anna Schultz 28 December 1896

---

[12] 1900 U.S. census, Worth County, Iowa, population schedule, Kensett Township, Enumeration District (ED) 149, p. 10-B, dwelling. 192, family 194, Harry B. King; imaged at *Ancestry* (https://www.ancestry.com/imageviewer/collections/7602/images/4120131_00137). 1910 U.S. census Worth County, Iowa, populations schedule, Grove, Enumeration District (ED) 172, pp. 4–5A, dwelling 63, family 67, H. B. King; imaged at *Ancestry* (http://www.ancestry.com: accessed 26 April 2018); citing NARA microfilm publication T624, roll 429. 1910 U.S. Federal Census (Population Schedule), Worth County, Iowa, Grove, ED 172, pp. 4–5A, dwelling, 63, family 67, H. B. King; imaged at *Ancestry* (https://www.ancestry.com/imageviewer/collections/7884/images/31111_4328324-00240). 1915 Iowa census, Worth County, Northwood Township, card no. 969, Harry B. King; imaged at *Ancestry* (https://www.ancestry.com/imageviewer/collections/1084/images/IA1915_533-4097). 1915 Iowa census, Worth County, Northwood Township, card no. 970, Anna King; imaged at *Ancestry* (https://www.ancestry.com/imageviewer/collections/1084/images/IA1915_533-4097).

[13] "Death Notice," *Worth County News,* 12 June 1919.

[14] "Obituary," *Worth County News,* Northwood, Iowa, 12 June 1919. Also, "Obituary," *Northwood Anchor,* Northwood, Iowa, 11 June 1919, p.1.

- Harry and Anna had five children: a son who died in infancy, and four daughters who survived, Ruby (Mrs. C. C. Miller), Rose, Ruth, and Rena.
- Farmed until about 1913, when he came to Northwood County and opened a confectionary

Harry Bernard King's footprints were not found in Virginia. His previous life story remained a mystery despite thirty-five years of documentary research in Virginia. Ultimately, DNA provided the key to Harry's origins. For an explanation of DNA see Appendix II.

DNA provides a link

Harry and Anna had four daughters but no surviving son; hence, Y-DNA testing could not be used to learn more about Harry.[15] Only one daughter, Ruby Anna King Miller, had biological children. Her two daughters are Betty Miller Francis and JoAnn Miller Eid.

On 3 August 2013, two years after Harry's granddaughters Betty and JoAnn, took the autosomal Family Finder test at Family Tree DNA, they received an e-mail from Kathy Weckwerth citing Family Finder DNA results showing a close cousin match within two generations to her brother, David Youmans. Dave matched Betty at 443 cM and JoAnn at 385 cM.[16] Kathy had prompted Dave to use DNA testing to attempt to learn the paternity of their grandfather, Herbert Youmans, born out of wedlock on 21 July 1897 in Iowa.[17]

---

[15] Y-DNA is passed only from father to sons, not to daughters. Autosomal DNA (atDNA) is passed from parents to all of their children.

[16] "Family Finder," database report, *Family Tree DNA* (http://familytreedna.com: accessed 23 August 2013), Matches for Betty include JoAnn and Dave; results from this dynamic database require a private passcode and kit number. E-mail correspondence with Youmans held privately by author.

[17] "WWI Draft Registration Cards, 1917–1918," imaged at *Ancestry* (https://www. ancestry.com/imageviewer/collections/2238/images/44018_10_00045-03336), Herbert Youmans. E-mail correspondence with Youmans held privately by author.

The King granddaughters told Kathy and Dave that in 1897 their only Iowa relatives were their grandparents, Harry King and Anna Schulz King, and their children.[18] Census records revealed that two Youmans families lived in Kensett at the same time Harry did. Both had teenaged girls in the household.[19]

---

[18] Betty Francis and JoAnn Eid, phone and E-mail communication with author, 2013.

[19] 1895 Iowa census, Worth County, Kensett Township, page 8, dwelling 40, family 41, B. B. Yomans imaged at *Ancestry* (https://www.ancestry.com/imageviewer/collections/1084/images/IA1885_416-0214). 1895 Iowa census, Worth County, Kensett Township, page 9, dwelling 48, family 46, Lafe Yomans imaged at *Ancestry* (https://www.ancestry.com/imageviewer/collections/1084/images/IA1885_416-0215).

Herbert Edgar Youmans

Emma Youmans, Kathy and Dave's unmarried great grandmother, left her infant son, Herbert Edgar Youmans, to be raised by his grandparents, Bennett Bicknell and Wallamette Youmans, farmers in Kensett, Worth County, Iowa.[20] Emma later married her first cousin John Youmans and moved to Waverly, Iowa, where she died following childbirth in August 1900.[21] According to Kathy and Dave, Herbert was unaware that his grandparents were not his parents. Shortly before 1920, the Youmans household, including Herbert, moved from Kensett, Iowa to Aitkin, Aitkin County, Minnesota because they had heard land was cheap.[22]

---

[20] 1900 U.S. census, Worth County, Iowa, population schedule, Kensett Township, Enumeration District (ED) 149, sheet 8-A, dwelling 156, family 157, Bennett Youmans; imaged at *Ancestry* (https://www.ancestry.com/imageviewer/collections/7602/images/4120131_00132). Herbert Youmans, 2, grandson, born July 1897, is enumerated in this household.

[21] 1900 U.S. census, Bremer County, Iowa, population schedule, Waverly Township, ED 37, sheet 15-B, dwelling 355, family 366, Emma Youmans; imaged at *Ancestry* (https://www.ancestry.com/imageviewer/collections/7602/images/4120097_00353). *Find A Grave*, database with images (https://www.findagrave.com/memorial/42857323), memorial for Emma Youmans (1879–1900), Harlington Cemetery, Waverly, Bremer County, Iowa.

[22] 1920 U.S. census Aitkin County, Minnesota, population schedule, Aitkin, Enumeration District (ED) 9, Sheet 13A, dwelling 141, family 142, Bennet

Herbert, 24, married Thelma Lucille Craig, 22, on 7 December 1921 in Aitkin, Minnesota. The bride was born 24 August 1899 in St. Charles, Saginaw County, Michigan, the daughter of William Mortimer Craig and Louisa "Lucy" Babion.[23]

A Kensett, Iowa, neighbor, Edna Hogan, also moved to Aitkin, MN.[24] Edna told Herbert's new wife the tale of Herbert's illegitimate birth and that Emma, the Youmans's oldest daughter, was Herbert's biological mother.[25] The gossip surrounding Herbert's paternity was that "the father was a riverboat gambler."

Herbert and Thelma raised two children in rural Aitkin, Duane, born in 1930, and Mary, born in 1937.[26] Herbert was an auto body

---

B. Youmans; imaged at *Ancestry* (https://www.ancestry.com/imageviewer/collections/6061/images/4311660-00195).

[23] "Minnesota Official Marriage System," database, Herbert Youmans and Thelma Craig, 7 December 1921, Aitkin County, Minnesota (https://moms.mn.gov/Search?S=1). For Thelma's parents see, 1900 U.S. census Saginaw County, Michigan, population schedule, St Charles Township, Enumeration District (ED) 74, Sheet 28-B, dwelling 582, family 589, William Craig; imaged at *Ancestry* (https://www.ancestry.com/imageviewer/collections/7602/images/4120252_00456).

[24] For Edna in Kensett, see 1910 U.S. census, Worth County, Iowa, population schedule, Kensett Town, Enumeration District (ED) 175, Sheet 4-A, dwelling 96, family 96, Frank Hogan; imaged at *Ancestry* (https://www.ancestry.com/imageviewer/collections/7884/images/31111_4328324-00289). For Edna in Aitkin, see 1930 U.S. census, Aitkin County, Minnesota, population schedule, Aitkin Village, Enumeration District (ED) 1-2, sheet 6-B, dwelling 141, family 142, Frank A Hogan; imaged at *Ancestry* (https://www.ancestry.com/imageviewer/collections/6224/images/4609318_00033).

[25] Kathy Weckwerth and Mary Elling Youmans E-mail correspondence with author 7/25/2020, privately held by author.

[26] 1940 U.S. census Aitkin County, Minnesota, population schedule, Aitkin Township, Enumeration District (ED) 1-1, Sheet 2-A, household 30, Louisa Craig;

mechanic by trade, but also a farmer and a trapper, and he drew maps for the county during the depression.[27] He died at age 48 on 24 April 1946.[28] Herbert's son Duane was father of Kathy Weckwerth and her brother, David Youmans, whose DNA matched Harry Bernard King's granddaughters. Duane Youmans passed away in February of 2009.[29]

---

imaged at *Ancestry* (https://www.ancestry.com/imageviewer/collections/2442/images/m-t0627-01903-00021).

[27] E-mail correspondence with Kathy Weckwerth 7/12/2020, privately held by author.

[28] "Minnesota, Death Index, 1908-2017," database, *Ancestry* (https://search.ancestry.com/cgi-bin/sse.dll?_phsrc=lyo781&_phstart=successSource&usePUBJs=true&indiv=1&dbid=7316&gsfn=herbert&gsln=youmans&msddy=1946&msdpn_ftp=aitkin,%20minnesota,%20usa&msdpn=123&new=1&rank=1&uidh=5ah&redir=false&msT=1&gss=angs-d&pcat=34&fh=0&h=2905847&recoff=&ml_rpos=1&queryId=fdf3080d5a920eec2dd9bf8b313388ef), Herbert Edgar Youmans, 24 April 1946, Aitkin County, Certificate Number 7, Record Number 1005618.

[29] "Obituary," *Clarinda Herald Journal*, Clarinda, Iowa, 16 Feb. 2009,

Additional DNA Link Discoveries

David Youmans tested his Y-DNA in August of 2013 but had only two matches at 25 markers.[30] He upgraded to 111 markers and the Big Y,[31] but the results showed no matches at 37, 67, or 111 markers.[32] Neither surname, King nor Youmans, appeared at any level. David joined surname projects Youmans/Yoemans and King, where he remained ungrouped.

---

[30] Y-DNA is passed only from father to sons, not to daughters. "Y-DNA Matches," database report, *FamilyTreeDNA* (http://familytreedna.com: accessed 10 May 2018), Dave (kit 264346); results from this dynamic database require a private passcode and kit number.

[31] The Big Y test scans the Y chromosome for mutations called SNPs, single nucleotide polymorphisms. SNPs define haplogroups and bring understanding of the migration patterns of our ancestors. David's test revealed new SNPs not found before, thereby extending the Y haplogroup tree. The results were completed 30 April 2014 and submitted to further testing by YFull. David's YFull number is YF20408.

[32] David's 37-marker Y-DNA results place him in haplogroup R-L21, also known as the "Little Scottish Cluster." After eliminating any possible connection to the maternal Germanic Schulz family, Harry King, a neighboring farmer recently from Virginia in 1894, remained the most likely match. David's Y-DNA at 37 markers had 0 matches; at 25 markers, 2 matches; at 12 markers, it produced 122 matches without a surname pattern. He joined project R-L21WtY and ordered R1b-L21v2 SNP pack.

David was upgraded for a mtDNA full sequence with the results in mtDNA haplogroup H26a, but the mtDNA is not significant for this study.

Dave's paternal aunt, Mary Youmans Elling, agreed to take the autosomal Family Finder test at FTDNA.[33] She was also a close match to the King granddaughters: 411 cM shared with Betty and 593 cM shared with JoAnn.

Everybody's results were uploaded to GEDmatch.com to enable direct comparisons. The kit numbers are Dave, Betty, and JoAnn,.[34] The GEDmatch.com Autosomal DNA comparison matrix showed a 443 cM match with Betty, with the largest block 69 cM, and a 402.2 cM match with JoAnn, with the largest block 71.2. These numbers are consistent with the expected half-first cousin once removed relationship.[35]

In March 2017, GEDmatch.com revealed a similarly close match to a tester who wishes to remain anonymous. "Participant X" matched Betty at 203.1 cM, JoAnn at 337.1 cM, David at 301.3cM, and Mary at 364.4 cM. The new match had posted her lineage in a family tree on Ancestry.[36] The tree showed that her great-grandfather, Charles

---

[33] FTDNA (www.ftdna.com) offers an autosomal DNA test that is known as "Family Finder." Autosomal DNA (atDNA) is passed from parents to all of their children, who then pass approximately half of it to their children, who pass a quarter to grandchildren, etc. DNA testing looks at genetic markers, specific locations on chromosomes where the constituent sequence of nucleotides can be observed. Similar sequences indicate similar heritage.

[34] If privacy is to be protected, these kit numbers must be deleted here, in footnote 40 and in table 1.

[35] Autosomal DNA analysis, on-request reports, *GEDmatch: Tools for DNA and Genealogy Research* (http://www.GEDMatch.com: accessed 3 August 2013), "One to Many" for kit T323600 (Dave) gives with matches to kit A062725 (Participant X), kit T333004 (Bob), kit T576400 (Betty), and T855174 (JoAnn), see table 1 under the heading of "DNA Analysis" for shared amounts of DNA.

[36] Participant X, Family Tree," *Ancestry* (http://www.Ancestry.com: accessed 27 March 2017), Charles E. Rinker. E-mail Correspondence with author, Sept.

Edwin Rinker, was born 17 December 1866, the same date as Harry Bernard King. Charles Rinker's mother died in 1871, when he was four, and his father died when he was sixteen. His grandmother was Anna Kingree Moore. This is nearly identical to the information in Harry Bernard King's obituary.

Participant X knew of no living Rinker male cousins to provide Y-DNA to confirm the probable match.

2017.

Charles Edwin Rinker

17 December 1866
Ashby, Shenandoah, Virginia

Charles E. Rinker was enumerated as a four-year-old in the 1870 U.S. Federal Census, Shenandoah County, Ashby Township, Virginia in the household of Erasmus Fayette Rinker and Elizabeth Sarah Moore.[37] The marriage bonds and records of Shenandoah County, Virginia, show that Erasmus F. Rinker and Elizabeth S. Moore were issued a marriage license on 5 May 1851 and were married on 8 May 1851 by John P. Cline. Those marriage records also show that Elizabeth Sarah Moore was a daughter of George Moore who married Ann Kingree, daughter of Solomon Kingree, on 21 April 1817 in Shenandoah County, Virginia.[38]

---

[37] 1870 U.S. census, Shenandoah County, Virginia, population schedule, Ashby Township, page 45, dwelling 341, family 339; imaged at *Ancestry* (https://www.ancestry.com/imageviewer/collections/7163/images/4268767_0004967.

[38] John Vogt and T. William Kethley, *Virginia Historic Marriage Register, Shenandoah County, Marriage Bonds, 1772-1850* (Athens, Georgia: Iberian Press, 1984), pp. 128-129, 134, 157, 316-317, 322, & 345-346.

Erasmus Rinker served as a commissioned officer in Company "G," Virginia, 136th Militia Infantry Regiment during the Civil War.[39] In 1860 Erasmus and wife Elizabeth farmed in Shenandoah County.[40] In 1870 son Charles, age 4, appeared with the family.[41] In 1880, Charles was 13 and Erasmus had a new wife, Josephine.[42]

Elizabeth Sarah Rinker, the mother of Charles Edwin Rinker, died when he was four years old, the same age Harry Bernard King said he was when his mother died. His grandmother's name was Anna Moore, the name he gave for his mother on his marriage record to Anna Schultz. [43] Erasmus Fayette Rinker died 18 February 1883, and his obituary appears in the *Rockingham Register* of Harrisonburg, Virginia. This obituary reports that the father of Erasmus died

---

[39] "Compiled Service Records of Confederate Soldiers Who Served in Organizations from the State of Virginia," imaged at *Fold3* (https://www.fold3.com/image/13455209), Erasmus F Rinker, Captain, Co G, 136 Virginia Militia (Confederate), five images.

[40] 1860 U.S. census, Shenandoah County, Virginia, population schedule, Ashby Township, page 205, dwelling 1380, family 1378, Erasmus Rinker; imaged at *Ancestry* (https://www.ancestry.com/imageviewer/collections/7667/images/4298872_00125).

[41] 1870 U.S. census, Shenandoah County, Virginia, population schedule, Ashby Township, page 45, dwelling 341, family 339, Erasmus Rinker; imaged at *Ancestry* (https://www.ancestry.com/imageviewer/collections/7163/images/4268767_00049).

[42] 1880 U.S. census, Shenandoah County, Virginia, population schedule, Ashby Township, Enumeration District (ED) 87, page 61-A, dwelling 474, family 516, Erasmus F Rinker; imaged at *Ancestry* (https://www.ancestry.com/imageviewer/collections/6742/images/4244638-00335).

[43] Shenandoah County, Virginia, Birth and Death Registers, 1853–1871, imaged at *FamilySearch* (https://www.familysearch.org/ark:/61903/3:1:3QS7-99XF-CKNS), Rinker, Eliz. Sarah, 9 February 1871. Entry lists her as the daughter of George and Anna Moore and the consort of Erasmus Rinker.

when he was fourteen years of age. [44] Erasmus wrote his will on 23 November 1879, it was proved on 12 March 1883, and it names Charles Rinker as his son.[45] So, Erasmus, the father of Charles E. Rinker, died when Charles was sixteen, but his grandfather died when Erasmus was fourteen.[46] Harry could very well have conflated the two stories when talking about being a teenager when his father died.

On 10 January 1884, nine months after his father died and one month past his 17th birthday, Charles Rinker was married to Emma Catherine Frye, aged 25, in Washington County, Maryland.[47] The bride was born 1 December 1858 to Moses Frye and his wife, Elizabeth, of Ashby, Shenandoah County, Virginia.[48] Emma was eight years and eleven months older than her 17-year-old groom.

Charles and Emma Rinker plunged into parenthood seven months later with the birth of a female "no name Rinker," on 12 August 1884, identified as Ethel Verne Rinker.[49] Three additional births

---

[44] "Died," *Rockingham Register*, Harrisonburg, Virginia, 15 March 1883.

[45] Shenandoah County, Virginia, Will Book 20, pages 138–139. Erasmus Fayette Rinker.

[46] Daniel Warrick Burris, II, *The Rinkers of Virginia* (Edinburg, VA: Shenandoah Historical Society, 1993), 66–67.

[47] "Washington County, Maryland, Marriage Index, 1861–1949," database, *Ancestry* (https://www.ancestry.com/discoveryui-content/view/7044:70012), Rinker - Frey 10 January 1884; citing Washington County Free Library (http://www.washcolibrary.org).

[48] "Virginia Death Records, 1912-2014," imaged at *Ancestry* (https://www.ancestry.com/discoveryui-content/view/7044:70012), Shenandoah County, Emma Rinker 10 December 1941.

[49] "Shenandoah County, Virginia Births, 1878-90," database, *Ancestry* (https://www.ancestry.com/search/collections/5074/), No Name Rinker (female), 12 August 1884. *Find A Grave*, (https://www.findagrave.com/memorial/62655008),

were registered to the couple: Edna Dare 1886, Nettie 1888, and Earl Edwin 1890.[50] Nettie remains a mystery since she disappears from records. In 1900, Emma was living in her father's farm household with those three children plus another daughter, Ella R. Rinker, born July 1892.[51] Ella's birth was not registered, nor is she named as one of Charles Rinker's children in the Rinker book.[52] By 1910, Emma was the owner and head of the farm household with the two youngest children, Earle E. and Ella, at home. Emma reported that she had 4 live births and 4 living children. Charles was absent.[53] This account appears in *The Rinkers of Virginia*:

> Charlie told his drinking buddies he was tired of married life and was going west; about the time his youngest child was born he disappeared from this area overnight, leaving his family behind. The year was 1890.

---

memorial 62655008, Ethel Verne Rinker Funkhouser, (1884-1941), Grace United Church of Christ Cemetery, Mount Jackson, Shenandoah County, Virginia.

[50] "Shenandoah County, Virginia Births, 1878-90," database, *Ancestry* (https://www.ancestry.com/search/collections/5074/), Edna Rinker, 5 August 1886. Ibid., Nettie Rinker, Sep 1888. Ibid., Earl Runker, 8 April 1890.

[51] 1900 U.S. census, Shenandoah County, Virginia, population schedule, Ashby, Enumeration District (ED) 72, sheet 4-B, dwelling 74, family 74, Moses Frey; imaged at *Ancestry* (https://www.ancestry.com/imageviewer/collections/7602/images/4117934_00012).

[52] Daniel Warrick Burris, II, *The Rinkers of Virginia* (Edinburg, VA: Shenandoah Historical Society, 1993), 66–67.

[53] 1910 U.S. census, Shenandoah County, Virginia, population schedule, Ashby, Enumeration District (ED) 86, sheet 6-B, dwelling 110, family 111, Emma Rinker; imaged at *Ancestry* (https://www.ancestry.com/imageviewer/collections/7884/images/4454833_01127).

Some years later, a stranger showed up one day at Pete Rinker's store at Rinkerton. After purchasing some cheese and crackers, he struck up a conversation with Pete Rinker. He subtly steered the conversation around to Charlie Rinker's wife and children, inquiring about their welfare and what they were doing. Pete Rinker took a closer look at the stranger, and even though he had aged, and wore a heavy beard, he recognized him. After about twenty to thirty minutes of conversation, Charlie left, went to Mt. Jackson and caught the train, and was never seen again.[54]

\Where did Charlie go? On 18 September 1892 in St. Joseph County, Indiana, one Charles E. Rinker married Alma Blanche Krou, a daughter of Jacob Krou and Ruth Moon.[55] Steven Lee Krou, family historian, provided a three-generation report which included this account of the short-lived Krou-Rinker marriage: "Shortly before their son Frederick was born, his first and legal wife from Virginia showed up and they had three children back in Virginia. Charlie took off never to be heard from again."[56] Alma, described as widowed, worked as a servant until she remarried, moved to Montana, and died young.[57] In the 1900 census, Frederick Rinker, age 6, was enumerated

---

[54] Daniel Warrick Burris, II, *The Rinkers of Virginia* (Edinburg, VA: Shenandoah Historical Society, 1993), 182.

[55] "Indiana Marriages, 1811–2007," imaged at *FamilySearch* (https://www.familysearch.org/ark:/61903/3:1:33S7-8BLN-9H34), St. Joseph County, Rinker-Krou, 18 September 1892.

[56] E-mail correspondence with Steven Lee Krou, April 2017, privately held by the author.

[57] 1900 U.S. census, St Joseph County, Indiana, populations schedule, Liberty, Enumeration District (ED) 105, sheet 9-A, dwelling 153, family 153, Henry

with his maternal grandparents; his father's birth location is listed as Virginia.[58] In 1910, Frederick, age 16, was still living with his grandparents in St. Joseph County, Indiana.[59] Frederick, son of Charles and Alma Krou Rinker, married, worked as a mail carrier in Chadron, Nebraska, and had three children, Genevieve, Richard and Robert. [60] He died in Nebraska in 1986.[61]

Hawblitzel; imaged at *Ancestry* (https://www.ancestry.com/imageviewer/collections/7602/images/4118654_00119). Elma B. Krow, 26, is a servant in the household. For marriage, see "Montana, U.S., County Marriages, 1865–1987," imaged at *Ancestry* (https://www.ancestry.com/imageviewer/collections/61578/images/48279_555201-00171), Valley County, Judson-Krou, 24 February 1921. For death, see "Montana, U.S., State Deaths, 1907–2016," imaged at *Ancestry* (https://www.ancestry.com/imageviewer/collections/5437/images/47791_1220706333_0779-00368), Valley County, Elma B Marks, 2 July 1929.

[58] 1900 U.S. census, St. Joseph County, Indiana, population schedule, Lakeville, Enumeration District (ED) 138, sheet 2-A, dwelling 28, family 28, Jacob Krou; imaged at *Ancestry* (https://www.ancestry.com/imageviewer/collections/7602/images/4118655_00493).

[59] 1910 U.S. census, St. Joseph County, Indiana, population schedule, Lakeville, Enumeration District (ED) 194, sheet 2-A, dwelling 41, family 42, Jacob Krow; imaged at Ancestry (https://www.ancestry.com/imageviewer/collections/7884/images/31111_4328272-00743).

[60] "South Dakota, U.S., Marriages, 1905-2017," imaged at *Ancestry* (https://www.ancestry.com/imageviewer/collections/8561/images/SDVR_M_24-0889), Fall River County, Rinker-Lefler 1 June 1931. Also, 1940 U.S. census, Dawes County, Nebraska, population schedule, Whitney, Enumeration District (ED) 23-18, sheet 2-A, household 27, Fred R. Rinker; imaged at Ancestry (https://www.ancestry.com/imageviewer/collections/2442/images/m-t0627-02243-00577).

[61] *Find A Grave* (https://www.findagrave.com/memorial/73390844/frederick-raymond-rinker), memorial 73390844, Frederick Raymond "Fred" Rinker (1893–1986), Whitney Cemetery, Whitney, Dawes County, Nebraska, gravestone photo by Kristal K.

Steve Krou also suggested the Zanabeth1 Family Tree on Ancestry, which provided a link to Robert "Bob" Rinker, an 82-year-old living son of Frederick and grandson of Charles E. Rinker.[62] Bob Rinker reports that life was very hard for his father, Fred, who lived with his grandparents until he was of age. Bob agreed to do DNA testing.[63] On 23 June 2017 Bob's DNA results showed that he is a half-first cousin once removed to Betty, JoAnn, David Youmans, Mary Youmans Elling, and Participant "X." Bob's Y-DNA is David Youmans only match. This is strong support that Charles Edwin Rinker in Virginia is the same person as Charles Edwin Rinker in Indiana and is the same person as Harry Bernard King in Worth County, Iowa.

---

[62] Correspondence with Steve Krou and others regarding "Zanabeth1 Family Tree," privately held by author.

[63] Bob Rinker and daughter Barbara Rinker Fann, E-mail correspondence, 2017, privately held by author.

Autosomal DNA Analysis

The following relationships are hypothesized among the participants. Analysis of the DNA confirms the likelihood of these relationships in **Figure: 1.**

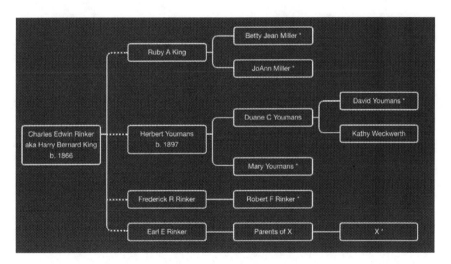

Several of these cousins should be half-first cousins, and two should be half-first cousins once removed.

The following chart shows the amount of DNA shared, according to GEDmatch, by the various descendants of Charles Edwin Rinker/ Harry Bernard King in **Figure 2:** [64]

Table 1 Shared Total Amount of atDNA Ver: Mar 27 2017 18:41:59 Value shown is cM total of matching segments over minimum threshold.							
Kit AKA	name	B	A	C	D	E	F
A	*David		2026.1	473.9	468.5	402.2	301.3
B	*Mary	2026.1		487.4	422.6	618.0	361.4
C	*Bob	473.9	487.4		426.1	379.2	256.8
D	*Betty	468.5	422.6	426.1		2753.4	203.1
E	*JoAnn	402.2	618.0	379.2	2753.4		337.1
F	*X	301.3	361.4	256.8	203.1	337.1	

Participants and relationship:

JoAnn, granddaughter of Harry Bernard King and sister of Betty Share 2573 cM

Betty, granddaughter of Harry Bernard King and sister of JoAnn Share 2573 cM

David, great grandson of Emma Youmans and unknown male Share 2026 cM with his aunt Mary

Mary, granddaughter of Emma Youmans and unknown male shares 422.6 cM with Betty

Participant X, great-granddaughter of Charles Edwin Rinker and Catherine Fry of Virginia shares 337 cM with Betty

---

[64] Autosomal DNA analysis, on-request reports, *GEDmatch: Tools for DNA and Genealogy Research* (http://www.GEDMatch.com: accessed 5 July 2017), "One to Many" for kit T323600 (David) with matches to kit A062725 (X), kit T333004 (Bob), kit T576400 (Betty), and T855174 (JoAnn).

Bob, grandson of Charles Edwin Rinker and Alma B. Krou of Indiana shares 426 cM with Betty,

FTDNA provided more details and estimated that Bob was a first cousin to second cousin match to Dave with 464 cM (largest segment 177 cM), Betty with 426.1 cM (largest segment 95.2 cM), JoAnn with 379.2 cM (largest segment 62.4 cM) and Participant X with 256.8 cM (largest segment 71.6 cM).[65]

If Harry was the mystery father of Herbert Youmans, Herbert's daughter Mary would be Harry's granddaughter and a half-first cousin to Betty and JoAnn. According to the Shared cM Tool on DNA Painter, as shown in the following tables, this relationship was consistent with the amount of DNA shared.[66]

Mary & Betty share 422 cM (on GEDmatch) and a half-first cousin relationship falls in the 80% probability box, **Figure 4:**

---

[65] FTDNA and GEDmatch use different algorithms to calculate the amount of shared DNA, so discrepancies are expected.

[66] DNA Painter conclusions thanks to Dr. Maurice Gleeson.

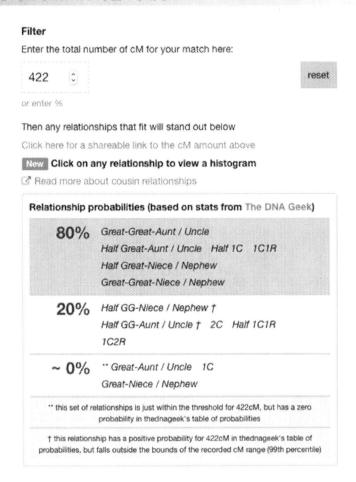

The overwhelmingly most probable relationship between Mary and Betty is half-first cousins, with Harry Bernard King being the grandfather of both.

Mary & JoAnn share 618 cM (on GEDmatch) and a half-first cousin relationship falls in the 69% probability box, **Figure 5:**

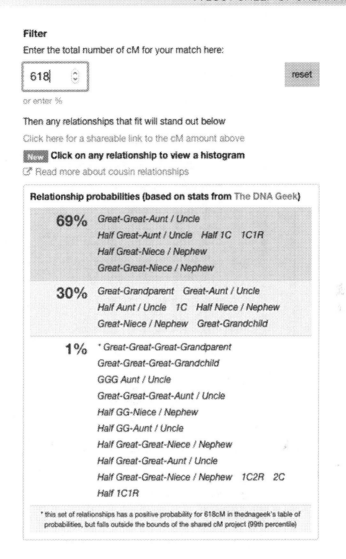

Filter

Enter the total number of cM for your match here:

618

reset

or enter %

Then any relationships that fit will stand out below

Click here for a shareable link to the cM amount above

New **Click on any relationship to view a histogram**

Read more about cousin relationships

Relationship probabilities (based on stats from The DNA Geek**)**

69% *Great-Great-Aunt / Uncle*
Half Great-Aunt / Uncle   Half 1C   1C1R
Half Great-Niece / Nephew
Great-Great-Niece / Nephew

30% *Great-Grandparent   Great-Aunt / Uncle*
Half Aunt / Uncle   1C   Half Niece / Nephew
Great-Niece / Nephew   Great-Grandchild

1% ** Great-Great-Great-Grandparent*
Great-Great-Great-Grandchild
GGG Aunt / Uncle
Great-Great-Great-Aunt / Uncle
Half GG-Niece / Nephew
Half GG-Aunt / Uncle
Half Great-Great-Niece / Nephew
Half Great-Great-Aunt / Uncle
Half Great-Great-Niece / Nephew   1C2R   2C
Half 1C1R

* this set of relationships has a positive probability for 618cM in thednageek's table of probabilities, but falls outside the bounds of the shared cM project (99th percentile)

The most significantly probable relationship between Mary and JoAnn is also half-first cousins, with Harry Bernard King being the grandfather of both.

If Harry and Charles were the same person, Bob Rinker would be a grandson and a half-first cousin to Betty, JoAnn and Mary. Bob shares 426 cM with Betty, 379 cM with JoAnn and 487 cM with Mary generating probabilities of 81%, 68% and 89% that they are half-first cousins. The overwhelmingly most probable relationship between Bob and Mary, Betty and JoAnn is half-first cousins, with Harry Bernard King aka Charles Edwin Rinker being the grandfather of all.

If Harry and Charles were the same person, Participant X would be a great granddaughter and a half-first cousin once removed to Betty, JoAnn, Mary and Bob. She shares 203 cM with Betty, 337 cM with JoAnn, 361 cM with Mary, and 256 cM with Bob generating probabilities of 46%, 46%, 39% and 62% that they are indeed half-first cousins once removed. These percentages are not as strong as the previous ones and indicate that Participant X received different Rinker DNA than the others, but the hypothesis that Harry Bernard King and Charles Edwin Rinker are the same person is still supported.

And finally, if Harry and Charles were the same person, David would also be a great grandson and a half-first cousin once removed to Betty, JoAnn and Bob. In addition, he would be a second cousin to Participant X. David shares 468.5 cM with Betty (largest segment 69 cM), 402.2 cM with JoAnn (largest segment 71.2 cM), and 473 cM with Bob generating probabilities of 9%, 25%, and 8 % that they are half-first cousin once removed.[67] These percentages indicate that David received similar Rinker DNA to the others. In contrast, he

---

[67] Diahan Southard, www.yourDNAguide.com, a well-known genealogical DNA forensics professional, was asked to evaluate the DNA evidence and reported that the results were generally in line with expected results for half-first cousins once removed (475 cM shared DNA), although David Youmans results were perhaps a bit stronger indicating perhaps an additional common ancestor. The 9 cM X-DNA common results for Betty and David Youmans is below the threshold of significance. X-DNA is peculiar in that it does not change from recombination, tiny identical segments can be considered indicative of ancestral roots in the distant past.

shares 301 cM with Participant X resulting in a probability of 57% that they are second cousins.

In summary, the autosomal DNA provides strong evidence that Harry Bernard King and Charles Edwin Rinker were the same person.

Y-DNA

Since two of the participants are patrilineal descendants of Charles Edwin Rinker/ Harry Bernard King, it was possible to compare the Y-DNA.

Dave Youman's Y-DNA falls into haplogroup R-M269 and is further refined to R-BY25635 with terminal SNP 111 marker FGC11134.[68] Bob Rinker's Y-DNA falls into the same categories. According to FTDNA, Dave has only 1 match at the 37-, 67- and 111-marker levels of comparison: Bob Rinker.

- The Genetic Distance between Dave and Bob is 2/111 (i.e., 2 mutations or "steps" away from an exact match on the 111

---

[68] In 2013 Ray Murta, R-L21 Group Administrator, wrote, "I've accessed David Youmans' Raw Data and uploaded it to the R-L21 Yahoo Project Big Y results file. His Big Y matches don't reveal any close relatives. It's interesting that their ancestors emigrated from Switzerland, and their line appears to have separated from the rest of the FGC11134 group immediately after that SNPs emergence. FGC11134 event occurred immediately downstream of DF13 at about the same time as the Celtic migration to the Isles. A debate currently taking place is whether DF13 originated on the continent or in the (British) Isles. The vast majority of the FGC11134 members in Alex's Tree are from the Isles." Alex is an administrator of the FGC11134 group.

STR markers of the Y-DNA test.)[69] Furthermore, they differ by only one additional mutation on the 431 STR markers added by the Big Y-500 test.[70]

- FTDNA reports that David has no Private Variants and Bob Rinker has one Private SNP (at position 10148841) - this too suggests a very close relationship.

- Another FTDNA report, the TiP Report, predicts Dave and Bob have a common ancestor within the last 4 generations (>85% probability).

These results can be seen in the R-FGC11134 and Subclades Project (kits numbered 264346 and 694826).[71]

The Y-DNA strengthens the argument presented by the genealogical records and the autosomal DNA that Harry Bernard King and Charles Edwin Rinker were the same man.

---

[69] A genetic distance of 2 in a 111-marker Y-DNA test means that the two men are closely related, i.e. 90% likelihood of a common male ancestor within 9 generations.

[70] On 27 Sep 2017, Ray Murta wrote: "I was recently requested "to compare the DNA results of one (Dave) and a match found through DNA testing (Bob). They have both taken the Big Y. . . . Analysis of the BAM file show that both Bob and Dave are positive for FGC11134 and FGC12055 and share a further 39 Variants reported in Dave's Novel Variants results. Dave has one additional Variant, 8253714 G.T. Bob's BAM file confirms that he is ancestral for this Variant, so a new branch is formed (which explains the absence of Y-DNA matches)," correspondence privately held by author. A BAM file is compressed sequenced DNA data.

[71] https://www.familytreedna.com/public/R-FGC11134?iframe=yresults.

A Lost Sheep of Shenandoah was Found

From the above, we can conclude the following:

1. The genealogical data indicates that Charles Edwin Rinker was married twice and the DNA match between the descendants of these marriages (Bob & X) confirms the expected relationship of half-first cousin once removed.[72]
2. Youmans strongly supports the contention that Charles Edwin Rinker was the mystery father of David's grandfather Herbert Youmans.
3. The autosomal DNA matches of the King sisters to Bob, David and Participant X supports the contention that their grandfather Harry Bernard King was in fact Charles Edwin Rinker. The "What Are The Odds" (WATO) tool can further strengthen that contention.

All the autosomal DNA results (from GEDmatch) were fed into the WATO tool on the DNAPainter website (https://dnapainter.com/tools/wato). Separate analyses were done for Betty & JoAnn to test for consistency. Hypotheses were created for Betty / JoAnn (Hypothesis 2), their mother Ruby (Hypothesis 1), a simulated child of Betty or JoAnn (Hypothesis 3), and a simulated grandchild (Hypothesis 4).

Betty's analysis shows that of the 4 hypothetical relationships to the others in the group, the most likely is Hypothesis 2 (which is exactly where Betty sits in the hypothetical tree). Hypothesis 4 is

---

[72] Note that Bob and X share 256 cM, consistent with a half-first cousin once removed relationship (which falls into the 62% probability box on the Shared cM Tool.)

not possible. Hypothesis 2 has a combined Odds Ratio of 32,726 in **Figure 6 and 7:**

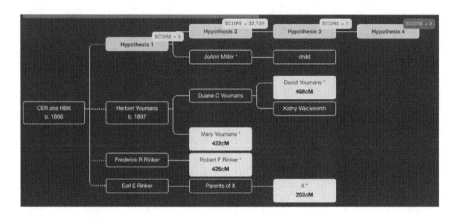

Match name	Shared cM	Hyp. 1	Hyp. 2	Hyp. 3	Hyp. 4
David Youmans *	468	Half Great-Aunt / Uncle 89.00%	Half 1C1R 5.10%	Half 2C 0.05%	Half 2C1R 0.00%
Robert F Rinker *	426	Half Aunt / Uncle 1.00%	Half 1C 88.60%	Half 1C1R 8.60%	Half 1C2R 0.10%
Mary Youmans *	422	Half Aunt / Uncle 1.00%	Half 1C 88.20%	Half 1C1R 9.20%	Half 1C2R 0.20%
X *	203	Half Great-Aunt / Uncle 8.60%	Half 1C1R 68.00%	Half 2C 20.93%	Half 2C1R 1.47%
Combined odds ratio		**9.24**	**32725.58**	**1.00**	**0.00**

JoAnn's analysis shows that of the 4 hypothetical relationships to the others in the group, the most likely is Hypothesis 2 (which is exactly where JoAnn sits in the hypothetical tree). Hypothesis 4 is not possible (score = 0). Hypothesis 2 has a combined Odds Ratio of 455,232. **See Figure 8 and 9:**

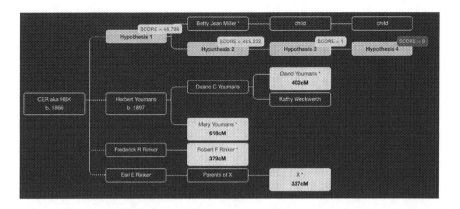

Match name	Shared cM	Hyp. 1	Hyp. 2	Hyp. 3	Hyp. 4
Mary Youmans *	618	Half Aunt / Uncle 47.50%	Half 1C 51.50%	Half 1C1R 0.50%	Half 1C2R 0.00%
David Youmans *	402	Half Great-Aunt / Uncle 85.40%	Half 1C1R 12.20%	Half 2C 0.50%	Half 2C1R 0.00%
Robert F Rinker *	379	Half Aunt / Uncle 0.73%	Half 1C 79.70%	Half 1C1R 18.40%	Half 1C2R 0.50%
X *	337	Half Great-Aunt / Uncle 62.85%	Half 1C1R 34.50%	Half 2C 0.83%	Half 2C1R 0.00%
Combined odds ratio		48706.06	455231.91	1.00	0.00

These WATO analyses, taken together with the genealogical evidence, strongly support the contention that Harry Bernard King and Charles Edwin Rinker are the same person.[73] *A lost sheep discovered by DNA.*

---

[73] Thanks to Dr. Maurice Gleeson, internationally known Y-DNA specialist, for his analysis of the probabilities and use of the WATO tool. WATO stands for What Are The Odds.

Conclusion

Charles Edwin Rinker was born in Ashby, Shenandoah, Virginia on 17 December 1866. His mother died when he was four; his father was an officer in the confederacy and died when Charles was sixteen. His father's father died when his father was fourteen. His grandmother was Anna Kingree Moore. Charles Edwin Rinker married Emma Catherine Frye at age 17, had three children, and he disappeared from Virginia around 1890.

Charles Edwin Rinker first appeared on record in St. Joseph County, Indiana, married Alma Blanche Krou on 18 September 1892, fathered a son Frederick, born 1 September 1893 (whose grandson Bob tested his Y-DNA), and disappeared shortly before Frederick was born.

Harry Bernard King was born 17 December 1866 in Virginia. He said his mother was Anna Moore, who died when he was four, and his father, who was an officer in the confederacy, died when he was fourteen. He married Anna Schulz on 28 December 1896 in Iowa, and fathered Ruby Anna King, born in June 1898 (whose granddaughters Betty and JoAnn tested autosomal DNA.) The 1900 and 1910 censuses confirm these wives and children.

Harry Bernard King fathered an illegitimate child, Herbert Youmans, born on 21 July 1897 (therefore conceived late October 1896, two months before the marriage to Anna Shultz). Y-DNA test participant David Youmans is Herbert's grandson.

Charles Rinker disappears from records in Shenandoah County, Virginia before appearing in Indiana. Rinker then disappears from records in Indiana before Harry King appears in Iowa. No earlier records for Harry Bernard King can be found anywhere. Together, the DNA and the documentary evidence leads to the conclusion that these are both the same man.

Charles Rinker abandoned two families, created a new identity by changing his name to Harry King, impregnated a young woman shortly before he married and started yet another family. But Charlie could not change his DNA. If he was a wolf in sheep's clothing, the Lost Sheep was found through DNA. His descendants are delighted to have found each other.

Appendix I

Lineages of participants

Harry Bernard King
m. 3 Anna Schulz

Charles Edwin Rinker
m2. Alma Blanche Krou

Harry Bernard King
u3. Emma Youmans

Ruby Anna King
m. Coy C. Miller

Frederick Raymond Rinker
m. Ellen Sarah Lefler

Herbert Edgar Youmans
m. Thelma Lucille Craig

Betty Jean Miller*,
JoAnn Miller

Robert Frederick Rinker

Duane C Youmans,
Mary Youmans

Appendix II

What is DNA ?

What is DNA? How does it work? To gain an overview of DNA, Google the website FamilyTreeDNA.com. They have the most comprehensive DNA resources of all the major companies; only FTDNA offers YDNA, the link from father to grandfather, to direct past paternal generations. The Family Finder test is autosomal, called atDNA. The atDNA test is a breakthrough test that reveals maternal DNA as well as paternal DNA through six past generations. The DNA divides as it passes down from one generation to the next, The amount of genetic DNA is measured in Centimorgans (cM). One centimorgan equals a one percent chance that a marker on a chromosome will become separated. YDNA is measured in markers that show mutations of the DNA changes.

Acknowledgements

The author would like to thank the following genealogists for assisting in her attempt to find a documentary record for Harry in Virginia over a period of thirty-five years: George Ott, Raquel Lindaas, Jane Bauer, Jane E. Sherman, Diahan Southard, Dr. Maurice Gleeson, Barbara Vines Little, Annette Burke Lyttle, and Ronald S. Beatty. For details, see client reports by these genealogists personally held by the author. Thanks to the helpful Shenandoah Historical Society for sending copies of wills.

Participants written permissions to publish the research are in the possession of the author.

Selected Bibliography and End Notes

WWW. Ancestry.com Anna's mother, Barbara Schultz, was a daughter of Peter Wagner as shown by her death record and several census records. *"Iowa, U.S., Death Records, 1920–1967,* imaged at *Ancestry* (https://www.ancestry.com/imageviewer/collections/61442/images/101784610 00426), Worth County, Mrs. Barbara Wagner Schultz, 13 May 1925.

1870 U.S. census, Dane County, Wisconsin, population schedule, Springfield, page 27, dwelling 170, family 170, Peter Wagner; imaged at *Ancestry* (https://www.ancestry.com/imageviewer/collections/7163/images/4268454 00416).

1880 U.S. census, Mitchell County, Iowa, population schedule, Osage Township, Enumeration District (ED) 309, page 10-B, dwelling 91, family 94, Peter E. Wagner; imaged at *Ancestry* (https://www.ancestry.com/imageviewer/collections/6742/images/4240928-00529).

1885 Iowa census, Mitchell County, Cedar Township, page 50, dwelling 66, family 1, Peter Wagner; imaged at *Ancestry* (https://www.ancestry.com/imageviewer/collections/1084/images/IA1885_234-0043).

Floyd County, Iowa, Marriage Record "G", Page 536; Marriage Register & Index 1896-1900, Page 139

1880 U.S. census, Dane County, Wisconsin, population schedule, Springfield Town, Enumeration District (ED) 89, page 23, dwelling 181, family 189, Carl Schulz; imaged at Ancestry (https://www.ancestry.com/imageviewer/collections/6742/images/4244707-00344). Also, 1895 Iowa census, Worth County, Kensett Township, page 11, dwelling 51, family 52, Carl Schultz; imaged at *Ancestry* (https://www.ancestry.com/imageviewer/collections/1084/images/IA1885_416-0217).

Find-A-Grave, Anna Schultz King Painter memorial: *Find-A-Grave* (https://www.findagrave.com/memorial/80960536: accessed July 2020), memorial for Anna Shultz Painter, (28 February 1877-19 April 1941), Sunset Rest Cemetery, Northwood, Worth County, Iowa.

"Iowa, U.S., Marriage Records, 1880–1951," Floyd County, King-Schultz, 26 December 1896; imaged at *Ancestry* (https://www.ancestry.com/imageviewer/collections/8823/images/42563_fp030872_0093-00211).

1900 U.S. census, Worth County, Iowa, population schedule, Kensett Township, Enumeration District (ED) 149, p. 10-B, dwelling. 192, family 194, Harry B. King; imaged at *Ancestry* (https://www.ancestry.com/imageviewer/collections/7602/images/4120131_00137).

1910 U.S. census Worth County, Iowa, populations schedule, Grove, Enumeration District (ED) 172, pp. 4–5A, dwelling 63, family 67, H. B. King; imaged at *Ancestry* (http://www.ancestry.com: accessed 26 April 2018); citing NARA microfilm publication T624, roll 429.

1910 U.S. Flederal Census (Population Schedule), Worth County, Iowa, Grove, ED 172, pp. 4–5A, dwelling, 63, family 67, H. B. King; imaged at *Ancestry* (https://www.ancestry.com/imageviewer/collections/7884/images/31111_4328324-00240).

1915 Iowa census, Worth County, Northwood Township, card no. 969, Harry B. King; imaged at *Ancestry* (https://www.ancestry.com/imageviewer/collections/1084/images/IA1915_533-4097).

1915 Iowa census, Worth County, Northwood Township, card no. 970, Anna King; imaged at *Ancestry* (https://www.ancestry.com/imageviewer/collections/1084/images/IA1915_533-4097).

"Death Notice," *Worth County News,* 12 June 1919.

"Obituary," *Worth County News,* **Northwood, Iowa**, 12 June 1919. Also, "Obituary," *Northwood Anchor,* Northwood, Iowa, 11 June 1919, p.1.

"Family Finder," database report, *Family Tree DNA* (http://familytreedna.com: accessed 23 August 2013), Matches for Betty include JoAnn and Dave; results from this dynamic database require a private passcode and kit number. E-mail correspondence with Youmans held privately by author.

"WWI Draft Registration Cards, 1917–1918," imaged at *Ancestry* (https://www.ancestry.com/imageviewer/collections/2238/images/44018_10_00045-03336), Herbert Youmans. E-mail correspondence with Youmans held privately by author.

Francis, Betty Miller and Eid JoAnn Miller, phone and E-mail communication with author, 2013.

1895 Iowa census, Worth County, Kensett Township, page 8, dwelling 40, family 41, B. B. Yomans imaged at *Ancestry* (https://www.ancestry.com/imageviewer/collections/1084/images/IA1885 416-0214).

1895 Iowa census, Worth County, Kensett Township, page 9, dwelling 48, family 46, Lafe Yomans imaged at *Ancestry* (https://www.ancestry.com/imageviewer/collections/1084/images/IA1885 416-0215).

1900 U.S. census, Worth County, Iowa, population schedule, Kensett Township, Enumeration District (ED) 149, sheet 8-A, dwelling 156, family 157, Bennett Youmans; imaged at *Ancestry* (https://www.ancestry.com/imageviewer/collections/7602/images/4120131 00132). Herbert Youmans, 2, grandson, born July 1897, is enumerated in this household.

1900 U.S. census, Bremer County, Iowa, population schedule, Waverly Township, ED 37, sheet 15-B, dwelling 355, family 366, Emma Youmans; imaged at *Ancestry* (https://www.ancestry.com/imageviewer/collections/7602/images/4120097 00353).

Find A Grave, database with images (https://www.findagrave.com/memorial/42857323), memorial for Emma Youmans (1879–1900), Harlington Cemetery, Waverly, Bremer County, Iowa.

1920 U.S. census Aitkin County, Minnesota, population schedule, Aitkin, Enumeration District (ED) 9, Sheet 13A, dwelling 141, family 142, Bennet B. Youmans; imaged at *Ancestry* (https://www.ancestry.com/imageviewer/collections/6061/images/4311660-00195).

"Minnesota Official Marriage System," database, Herbert Youmans and Thelma Craig, 7 December 1921, Aitkin County, Minnesota (https://moms.mn.gov/Search?S=1). For Thelma's parents see, 1900 U.S. census Saginaw County, Michigan, population schedule, St Charles Township, Enumeration District (ED) 74, Sheet 28-B, dwelling 582, family 589, William Craig; imaged at *Ancestry* (https://www.ancestry.com/imageviewer/collections/7602/images/4120252_00456).

1910 U.S. census, Worth County, Iowa, population schedule, Kensett Town, Enumeration District (ED) 175, Sheet 4-A, dwelling 96, family 96, Frank Hogan; imaged at *Ancestry* (https://www.ancestry.com/imageviewer/collections/7884/images/31111_4328324-00289). For Edna in Aitkin, see 1930 U.S. census, Aitkin County, Minnesota, population schedule, Aitkin Village, Enumeration District (ED) 1-2, sheet 6-B, dwelling 141, family 142, Frank A Hogan; imaged at *Ancestry* (https://www.ancestry.com/imageviewer/collections/6224/images/4609318_00033).

Weckwerth, Kathy, and Elling, Mary Youmas, E-mail correspondence with author 7/25/2020, privately held by author.

1940 **U.S. census Aitkin County, Minnesota**, population schedule, Aitkin Township, Enumeration District (ED) 1-1, Sheet 2-A, household 30, Louisa Craig; imaged at *Ancestry* (https://www.ancestry.com/imageviewer/collections/2442/images/m-t0627-01903-00021).

Weckwerth, Kathy, E-mail correspondence 7/12/2020, privately held by author.

"Minnesota, Death Index, 1908-2017," database, *Ancestry* (https://search.ancestry.com/cgi-bin/sse.dll? phsrc=lyo781& phstart=successSource&usePUBJs=true&indiv=1&dbid=7316 &gsfn=herbert&gsln=youmans&msddy=1946&msdpn ftp=aitkin,%20minnesota,%20usa&msdpn=123&new=1 &rank=1&uidh=5ah&redir=false&msT=1&gss=angs-d& pcat=34&fh=0&h=2905847&recoff=&ml rpos=1&queryId=fdf30 80d5a920eec2dd9bf8b313388ef), Herbert Edgar Youmans, 24 April 1946, Aitkin County, Certificate Number 7, Record Number 1005618.

"Obituary," *Clarinda Herald Journal*, Clarinda, Iowa, 16 Feb. 2009,

FTDNA (www.ftdna.com) offers an autosomal DNA test that is known as "Family Finder." Autosomal DNA (atDNA) is passed from parents to all of their children, who then pass approximately half of it to their children, who pass a quarter to grandchildren, etc. DNA testing looks at genetic markers, specific locations on chromosomes where the constituent sequence of nucleotides can be observed. Similar sequences indicate similar heritage.

GEDmatch: Tools for DNA and Genealogy Research Autosomal DNA analysis, on-request reports, *GEDmatch: Tools for DNA and Genealogy Research* (http://www.GEDMatch.com: accessed 3 August 2013), "One to Many" for (Dave) gives with matches to (Participant X), kit (Bob), (Betty), and (JoAnn), see table 1 under the heading of "DNA Analysis" for shared amounts of DNA.

Participant X Family Tree," *Ancestry* (http://www.Ancestry.com: accessed 27 March 2017), Charles E. Rinker. E-mail Correspondence with author, Sept. 2017.

1870 U.S. census, Shenandoah County, Virginia, population schedule, Ashby Township, page 45, dwelling 341, family 339; imaged at *Ancestry* (https://www.ancestry.com/imageviewer/collections/7163/images/4268767_0004967.

Vogt, John and Kethley, T. William, *Virginia Historic Marriage Register, Shenandoah County, Marriage Bonds, 1772-1850* (Athens, Georgia: Iberian Press, 1984), pp. 128-129, 134, 157, 316-317, 322, & 345-346.

"Compiled Service Records of Confederate Soldiers Who Served in Organizations from the State of Virginia," imaged at *Fold3* (https://www.fold3.com/image/13455209), Erasmus F Rinker, Captain, Co G, 136 Virginia Militia (Confederate), five images.

1860 U.S. census, Shenandoah County, Virginia, population schedule, Ashby Township, page 205, dwelling 1380, family 1378, Erasmus Rinker; imaged at *Ancestry* (https://www.ancestry.com/imageviewer/collections/7667/images/4298872_00125).

1870 U.S. census, Shenandoah County, Virginia, population schedule, Ashby Township, page 45, dwelling 341, family 339, Erasmus Rinker; imaged at *Ancestry* (https://www.ancestry.com/imageviewer/collections/7163/images/4268767_00049).

1880 U.S. census, Shenandoah County, Virginia, population schedule, Ashby Township, Enumeration District (ED) 87, page 61-A, dwelling 474, family 516, Erasmus F Rinker; imaged at *Ancestry* (https://www.ancestry.com/imageviewer/collections/6742/images/4244638-00335).

Shenandoah County, Virginia, Birth and Death Registers, 1853–1871, imaged at *FamilySearch* (https://www.familysearch.org/ark:/61903/3:1:3QS7-99XF-CKNS), Rinker, Eliz. Sarah, 9 February 1871. Entry lists her as the daughter of George and Anna Moore and the consort of Erasmus Rinker.

"Died," *Rockingham Register*, **Harrisonburg, Virginia**, 15 March 1883.

Shenandoah County, Virginia, Will Book 20, pages 138–139. Erasmus Fayette Rinker.

Burris, Daniel Warrick II, *The Rinkers of Virginia* (Edinburg, VA: Shenandoah Historical Society, 1993), 66–67.

"Washington County, Maryland, Marriage Index, 1861–1949," database, *Ancestry* (https://www.ancestry.com/discoveryui-content/view/7044:70012), Rinker - Frey 10 January 1884; citing Washington County Free Library (http://www.washcolibrary.org).

"Virginia Death Records, 1912-2014," imaged at *Ancestry* (https://www.ancestry.com/discoveryui-content/view/7044:70012), Shenandoah County, Emma Rinker 10 December 1941.

"Shenandoah County, Virginia Births, 1878-90," database, *Ancestry* (https://www.ancestry.com/search/collections/5074/), No Name Rinker (female), 12 August 1884. *Find A Grave*, (https://www.findagrave.com/memorial/62655008), memorial 62655008, Ethel Verne Rinker Funkhouser, (1884-1941), Grace United Church of Christ Cemetery, Mount Jackson, Shenandoah County, Virginia.

"Shenandoah County, Virginia Births, 1878-90," database, *Ancestry* (https://www.ancestry.com/search/collections/5074/), Edna Rinker, 5 August 1886. Ibid., Nettie Rinker, Sep 1888. Ibid., Earl Runker, 8 April 1890.

1900 U.S. census, Shenandoah County, Virginia, population schedule, Ashby, Enumeration District (ED) 72, sheet 4-B, dwelling 74, family 74, Moses Frey; imaged at *Ancestry* (https://www.ancestry.com/imageviewer/collections/7602/images/4117934_00012).

Burris, Daniel Warrick, *The Rinkers of Virginia* (Edinburg, VA: Shenandoah Historical Society, 1993), 66–67.

1910 U.S. census, Shenandoah County, Virginia, population schedule, Ashby, Enumeration District (ED) 86, sheet 6-B, dwelling 110, family 111, Emma Rinker; imaged at *Ancestry* (https://www.ancestry.com/imageviewer/collections/7884/images/4454833_01127).

Burris, Daniel Warrick, II, *The Rinkers of Virginia* (Edinburg, VA: Shenandoah Historical Society, 1993), 182.

"Indiana Marriages, 1811–2007," imaged at *FamilySearch* (https://www.familysearch.org/ark:/61903/3:1:33S7-8BLN-9H34), St. Joseph County, Rinker-Krou, 18 September 1892.

Krou Steven Lee, E-mail correspondence with Steven Lee Krou, April 2017, privately held by the author.

1900 U.S. census, St Joseph County, Indiana, populations schedule, Liberty, Enumeration District (ED) 105, sheet 9-A, dwelling 153, family 153, Henry Hawblitzel; imaged at *Ancestry* (https://www.

ancestry.com/imageviewer/collections/7602/images/4118654 00119). Elma B. Krow, 26, is a servant in the household. For marriage, see:

"**Montana, U.S., County Marriages, 1865–1987,**" imaged at *Ancestry* (https://www.ancestry.com/imageviewer/collections/61578/images/48279 555201-00171), Valley County, Judson-Krou, 24 February 1921. For death, see:

"**Montana, U.S., State Deaths, 1907–2016,**" imaged at *Ancestry* (https://www.ancestry.com/imageviewer/collections/5437/images/47791 1220706333 0779-00368), Valley County, Elma B Marks, 2 July 1929.

1900 U.S. census, St. Joseph County, Indiana, population schedule, Lakeville, Enumeration District (ED) 138, sheet 2-A, dwelling 28, family 28, Jacob Krou; imaged at *Ancestry* (https://www.ancestry.com/imageviewer/collections/7602/images/4118655 00493).

1910 U.S. census, St. Joseph County, Indiana, population schedule, Lakeville, Enumeration District (ED) 194, sheet 2-A, dwelling 41, family 42, Jacob Krow; imaged at Ancestry (https://www.ancestry.com/imageviewer/collections/7884/images/31111 4328272-00743).

"**South Dakota, U.S., Marriages, 1905-2017,**" imaged at *Ancestry* (https://www.ancestry.com/imageviewer/collections/8561/images/SDVR M 24-0889), Fall River County, Rinker-Lefler 1 June 1931. Also, 1940 U.S. census, Dawes County, Nebraska, population schedule, Whitney, Enumeration District (ED) 23-18, sheet 2-A, household 27, Fred R. Rinker; imaged at Ancestry (https://www.ancestry.com/imageviewer/collections/2442/images/m-t0627-02243-00577).

Find A Grave (https://www.findagrave.com/memorial/73390844/
frederick-raymond-rinker), memorial 73390844, Frederick Raymond
"Fred" Rinker (1893–1986), Whitney Cemetery, Whitney, Dawes
County, Nebraska, gravestone photo by Kristal K.

Rinker, Bob, Fann, Barbara Rinker, E-mail correspondence, 2017,
privately held by author.

GEDmatch: Tools for DNA and Genealogy Research Autosomal
DNA analysis, on-request reports, *GEDmatch: Tools for DNA and
Genealogy Research* (http://www.GEDMatch.com: accessed 5 July
2017), "One to Many" for kit T323600 (David) with matches to kit
A062725 (X), kit T333004 (Bob), kit T576400 (Betty), and T855174
(JoAnn).

**Gleeson, Dr. Maurice, PhD. DNA Painter and WATO, What are
the Odds** conclusions thanks to Dr. Maurice Gleeson.

Southard, Diahan, www.yourDNAguide.com, a well-known
genealogical DNA forensics professional, was asked to evaluate the
DNA evidence and reported that the results were generally in line
with expected results for half-first cousins once removed (475 cM
shared DNA), although David Youmans results were perhaps a bit
stronger indicating perhaps an additional common ancestor. The
9 cM X-DNA common results for Betty and David Youmans is
below the threshold of significance. X-DNA is peculiar in that it
does not change from recombination, tiny identical segments can be
considered indicative of ancestral roots in the distant past.

Murta, Ray, 2013 Ray Murta, R-L21 Group Administrator, wrote,
"I've accessed David Youmans' Raw Data and uploaded it to the

R-L21 Yahoo Project Big Y results file. His Big Y matches don't reveal any close relatives. It's interesting that their ancestors emigrated from Switzerland, and their line appears to have separated from the rest of the FGC11134 group immediately after that SNPs emergence. FGC11134 event occurred immediately downstream of DF13 at about the same time as the Celtic migration to the Isles. A debate currently taking place is whether DF13 originated on the continent or in the (British) Isles. The vast majority of the FGC11134 members in Alex's Tree are from the Isles."

Alex is an administrator of the FGC11134 group.

A Lost Sheep of Shenandoah

Charles Edwin Rinker
1866-1919
Ancestral Lineage

1. Charles Edwin Rinker[1,2,3,4,5,6,7,8,9], son of **2. Erasmus Fayette Rinker** & **3. Elizabeth Sarah MOORE**. Born on 17 Dec 1866 in Shenandoah, Virginia, USA. Charles Edwin AKA Harry Bernard King, died in Northwood, Worth County, Iowa, on 6 Jun 1919; he was 52.[10] Born on 17 Dec 1866 in Ashby, Shenandoah, Virginia, USA.[1,2,3,4,5,6,11]. Buried in Northwood, Worth County, Iowa, USA.[4,12] On 23 MAY 1911, he was received in the United Methodist Church, Northwood, Iowa.

On 28 Dec 1896 when Harry AKA Charles Edwin was 30, he married **Anna Schulz**[1,13,14,15,16,17,18,19,20,21,22,23] at the Little Brown Church in the Vale, Charles City, Floyd County, Iowa.[24,13,2,12] To this union four daughters and a stillborn son were born: Ruby Anna, Rose Ellen, Ruth Irene, and Rena Bernice. [14,15,16,17,18,19,20,21,22,23]

Charles Edwin Rinker Changed His
Name to Harry Bernard King

One Man, Four Families: DNA Reveals Harry
Bernard King aka Charles Edwin Rinker

Harry Bernard King appeared in Worth County, Iowa, in 1894, about 27 years old. He married there in 1896 and had five children. His obituary in 1919 said he was born and raised in Virginia, but no documentary evidence was found for him in that state. DNA linked Harry to his Virginia origins under another name, along with two additional marriages and an illegitimate son.

GENERATION 2

Erasmus Fayette Rinker[25,26,27,28,29,30,31,32,33,34,35,36], son of **4. Ephraim Rinker** & **5. Anna Brock**. Born on 12 Oct 1824 in Shenandoah CO.[26,28,29,30,31,32] Erasmus Fayette died in Rockingham County, Virginia, USA, on 18 Feb 1883; he was 58.[26,27] Buried in Mount Clifton, Shenandoah County, Virginia, USA.[27]

On 8 May 1851 when Erasmus Fayette was 26, he married **Elizabeth Sarah MOORE**[37,38,39,33,40,41] in Shenandoah, Virginia, USA.[33]

3. Elizabeth Sarah MOORE[37,38,39,33,40,41], daughter of **6. George Moore** & **7. Anna Kingree**. Born on 30 May 1829 in Virginia.[38,42,39,40] Elizabeth Sarah died in Virginia on 9 Feb 1871; she was 41.[38] Elizabeth Sarah died in Virginia, USA, on 10 Feb 1871; she was 41. Born on 30 May 1829 in Virginia, USA. Buried in United States.[38]

58

Erasmus Fayette Rinker was born 12 October 1824, died 18 Feb. 1882; married 8 May 1851 Elizabeth Sarah, daughter of George and Anna (Kingree) Moore. Elizabeth Moore was born 10 May 1829, died 10 Feb. 1871; Erasmus and Elizabeth are buried at Walnut Grove, Virginia. They had ten children.

1. Anna Leila, b. 2 Feb. 1852, d. 22 Oct 1861, buried at Walnut Grove.
2. Mary Elizabeth, b. 22 Feb 1853, d. 23 Mar 1912, buried at Walnut Grove.
3. Milton Moore Rinker, b. 24 May 1854, d. 15 Oct 1854, buried at Walnut Grove.
4. Emma Eugenia Rinker, b. 8 Oct 1855, d. 6 Sep 1910, buried at Walnut Grove.
5. Ida Virginia Rinker, b. 30 Aug 1857, d. 31 May 1858, buried at Walnut Grove.
6. Cora Isminia (Minnie) Rinker, b. 28 Mar 1859, d. 20 Oct 1905, buried at Walnut Grove.
7. Alice Imogen Rinker, b. 19 Jul 1861, d. 16 Feb 1916, buried at Walnut Grove.
8. Ella Lee Rinker, b. 25 Aug 1863, d. 16 Feb 1916, buried at Walnut Grove.
9. Charles Edwin Rinker b. 17 Dec 1866 m. 10 Jan 1884 Emma Catherine, daughter of Moses Frye. The number of children Charles fathered with Emma is uncertain. An unnamed daughter b 10 Aug 1884; there is not a birth registration for Ethel Vherne enumerated in the 1900 US Federal Census, b. 12 Sep 1885, Edna Dare, 5 Aug 1886, Nettie, b. Sep 1888, but not enumerated in the 1900 Census, and Earl Edwin b. 8 Apr 1890. Included in the 1900 Census is a daughter Ella R

Rinker b. Jul 1892 – no birth registration was filed for Ella. Charles reportedly left Rinkerton in 1890.

10. Lillian Howard Rinker, b. 9 Aug 1858.

Erasmus F. Rinker served in Co. H, 12th Virginia Cavalry during the War. After Elizabeth Moore Rinker died 10 Feb 1871, Erasmus married Harriet J. Nichols 2 Dec 1872.

Erasmus F. Rinker's will is recorded in Shenandoah County Will Book 20, page 138. The will was dated 22 Nov 1879. *"My desk, watch, and gun to my son Charles."* Additionally Charles was given 120 acres of land on the farm adjoining the home place. The will was probated 12 Mar 1883. Erasmus' obituary The Rockingham Register, 15 March 1883, Harrisonburg, VA

Died near Lacy Springs, Rockingham, VA, 18 Feb 1883, Erasmus F. Rinker, Esq., age 58 years, 4 months and 5 days.

GENERATION 3

4. Ephraim Rinker[43,44,45,46,47,48,49,50,51,52,53,54,55,56,57,58], son of **8. Colonel Jacob Rinker** & **9. Mary Keller.** Born on 14 May 1788 in Virginia.[43,44,45,46,55,56] Ephraim died in, Shenandoah, Virginia, USA, on 12 Nov 1830; he was 42.[55,56] Buried in Mount Clifton, Shenandoah County, Virginia, USA.[56]

On 21 Apr 1818 when Ephraim was 29, he married **Anna Brock**[59,54,60,61,62,63,64,65] in Rockingham, Virginia.[50,54,55]

5. Anna Brock[59,54,60,61,62,63,64,65], daughter of **10. John Brock Sr & 11. Ann Jones**. Born on 4 Jun 1793 in, Shenandoah, Virginia, USA.[63] Anna died on 18 Apr 1850; she was 56.[63] Buried in Mount Clifton, Shenandoah County, Virginia, USA.[63] Born on 4 Jun 1793.

6. George Moore[66,67,68,69,70,71,72,73,74], son of **12. Joseph Moore & 13. Margaret Rader**. George died in Shenandoah County, Virginia, USA, on 10 May 1844; he was 54.[67] Born on 7 Nov 1789 in Virginia, United States.[67] Buried in Mount Jackson, Shenandoah County, Virginia, USA.[67] George died in Shenandoah County, Virginia, USA, on 10 May 1841; he was 51. George died in Shenandoah County, Virginia, USA, on 10 May 1841; he was 51.[72] Born abt 1785 in Virginia, United States.[68]

George married **Anna Kingree**[75,76,77,78,79] in Shenandoah, Virginia, United States.

7. Anna Kingree[75,76,77,78,79], daughter of **14. Solomon Kingrey & 15. Elizabeth Jones**. Born on 16 Dec 1798 in Shenandoah, Virginia, United States.[80,77] Anna died in Shenandoah, Virginia, United States, on 15 Feb 1854; she was 55. Buried in Mount Jackson, Shenandoah County, Virginia, USA.[80]

GENERATION 4

8. Colonel Jacob Rinker[81,82,83,84,85,86,87,88,89], son of **16. Hans Jacob Rinker Sr & 17. Ana Maria LNU**. Born on 28 Mar 1749 in Mt Olive, Shenandoah, Virginia, United States.[81,82,83,86] Colonel Jacob died in Woodstock, Shenandoah, Virginia, USA, on 18 Jan 1827; he was 77.[81,82,86] Buried in Conicville, Shenandoah County, Virginia, USA.[82]

On 3 May 1772 when Colonel Jacob was 23, he married **Mary Ke ller**[90,91,92,93,94,95,96] in Toms Brook, Shenandoah, Virginia, United States.[83,86]

9. Mary Keller[90,91,92,93,94,95,96], daughter of **18. George Keller**. Born on 1 Mar 1753 in Shenandoah Co,, Virginia, USA.[90,92,93,94,95] Mary died in, Greene, Tennessee, USA, on 15 Mar 1806; she was 53.[90,92,95] Buried in Conicville, Shenandoah County, Virginia, United States of America.[95]

10. John Brock Sr.[97,98,99,100,101] John died in Rockingham Va, on 17 Apr 1827; he was 73.[100] Born on 25 Jun 1753 in, Augusta, Virginia, USA.[100] Buried in Keezletown, Rockingham County, Virginia, USA.[100]

On 26 Nov 1782 when John was 29, he married **Ann Jones**[102,103,104] in Rockingham County, Virginia.[103]

11. Ann Jones[102,103,104], daughter of **22. Evans Jones**. Born on 11 Jun 1758 in Fort, Marshall, South Dakota, United States.[102] Ann died in Shenandoah, Virginia, United States, on 27 Nov 1827; she was 69.[102] Buried in Keezletown, Rockingham County, Virginia, USA.[102]

12. Joseph Moore[105,106,107], son of **24. Thomas Moore & 25. Mary Allen**. Born in 1752 in Orange, Orange, Virginia, United States. Joseph died in Shenandoah, Virginia, United States, on 12 Jun 1820; he was 68.

Joseph married **Margaret Rader**[108] in Shenandoah, Virginia, United States.

13. Margaret Rader[108], daughter of **26. George Rader Sr. & 27. Catherine Jones**. Born abt 1768 in Shenandoah, Virginia, United States. Margaret died in Shenandoah Co., VA, in 1803; she was 35.

14. Solomon Kingrey[109,110,111,112,113], son of **28. Daniel Kingerey & 29. Rosina**. Born in Virginia.[110,111]

Solomon married **Elizabeth Jones**.

15. Elizabeth Jones, daughter of **30. William Jones & 31. Elizabeth**.

GENERATION 5

16. Hans Jacob Rinker Sr[114], son of **32. Jakob Ringger & 33. Barbara Morff**. Born on 24 Sep 1724 in Switzerland. Hans Jacob died in Shenandoah County, Virginia, United States of America, on 26 Aug 1797; he was 72. Buried in Conicville, Shenandoah County, Virginia, United States of America. Born on 4 Sep 1724 in Nuerensdorf, Zürich, Switzerland.[115,116,117] Hans Jacob died in Cabin Hill, Shenandoah, VA, USA, on 26 Aug 1797; he was 72.[118,117] Buried in Conicville, Shenandoah County, Virginia, USA.[117]

Hans Jacob married **Ana Maria LNU** in of PA.[115]

17. Ana Maria LNU. Ana Maria died bef 1754.

18. George Keller.[119] Born on 17 May 1711.[119] George died in Shenandoah County, Virginia, United States of America, in 1782; he was 70.[119] Buried in Mount Olive, Shenandoah County, Virginia, United States of America.[119]

22. Evans Jones.[120]

24. Thomas Moore[121,122,123,124,125,126,127,128,129,130,131,132,133,134,135], son of **48. Thomas Moore**. Born in Mar 1712 in New Haven, New Haven, Connecticut, USA. Thomas died in Shenandoah, Virginia, United States, on 30 Dec 1790; he was 78.[132] Born on 1 Feb 1712 in Cecil, Maryland, United States.[122]

In 1737 when Thomas was 24, he married **Mary Allen**[136,137,138,139] in Frederick, Virginia, United States.[137]

25. Mary Allen[136,137,138,139], daughter of **50. Reuben Allen & 51. Mary Jackson**. Born in 1720 in Cecil, Maryland, United States.[137,138] Mary died in Shenandoah County, Virginia, USA, aft 1790; she was 70.[137]

26. George Rader Sr.[140,141,142,143,144,145], son of **52. Johan Adam Rader & 53. Anna Barbara Bender**. Born in 1743 in Bethlehem, Lehigh, Pennsylvania, United States.[141,144] George died in Greenbrier County, West Virginia, USA, on 24 Oct 1815; he was 72.[141]

In 1779 when George was 36, he married **Catherine Jones**[146] in Pennsylvania, Somerset, Pennsylvania, United States.

27. Catherine Jones.[146] Born in 1745 in Northampton, Northampton, Pennsylvania, United States. Catherine died in Rockingham, Virginia, United States, in 1786; she was 41.

28. Daniel Kingerey, son of **56. Christian Kingrey & 57. Elizabeth**. Born in 1728. Daniel died in 1808; he was 80.

Daniel married **Rosina**.

29. Rosina.

30. William Jones. William died in Shenandah Co, Va. in 1789.

William married **Elizabeth**.

31. Elizabeth.

GENERATION 6

32. Jakob Ringger[147,148,149,150,88,151], son of **64. Kunrad Ringger & 65. Anna Egolf**. Born in 1695 in Bassersdorf, Zurich, Switzerland.[148] Jakob died in Nuerensdorf, Zurich, Switzerland, on 24 Oct 1734; he was 39.

On 9 Jan 1720 when Jakob was 25, he married **Barbara Morff**[88,147,152] in Nürensdorf, Zurich, Switzerland.

33. Barbara Morff[88,147,152], daughter of **66. Jakob Morff & 67. Regula Binder**. Born on 19 Feb 1693 in Nuerensdorf, Zürich, Switzerland. Barbara died in Nuerensdorf, Zürich, Switzerland, on 26 Dec 1732; she was 39.

48. Thomas Moore.[153]

50. Reuben Allen[154], son of **100. Joseph Allen & 101. Abigaill Savell**. Born in 1698 in Sandwich, Barnstable, Massachusetts, United States. Reuben died in Augusta, Virginia, United States, in 1741; he was 43.

In 1720 when Reuben was 22, he married **Mary Jackson**[155] in Baltimore, Maryland, United States.

51. Mary Jackson.[155] Born in 1703 in Cecil, Baltimore, Maryland, United States. Mary died in Orange, Orange, Virginia, United States, on 29 May 1751; she was 48.

52. Johan Adam Rader[156,157,158,159], son of **104. Johann Adam Roder** & **105. Anna Katharina TAUBER**. Born on 2 Jul 1706 in Mutterstadt, Ludwigshafen, Rheinland-Pfalz, Germany.[160,157] Johan Adam died in Timberville, Rockingham, Virginia, United States, on 18 Apr 1773; he was 66.[161]

In Aug 1724 when Johan Adam was 18, he married **Anna Barbara Bender**[162,163] in, Montgomery, Pennsylvania, USA.

53. Anna Barbara Bender.[162,163] Born on 15 Nov 1708 in Illingen, Enzkreis, Baden-Wuerttemberg, Germany. Anna Barbara died in Timberville, Rockingham, Virginia, United States, in 1773; she was 64.

56. Christian Kingrey. Christian died in Lancaster Co, PA.

Christian married **Elizabeth**.

57. Elizabeth.

GENERATION 7

64. Kunrad Ringger[164], son of **128. Jog li Ringger** & **129. Elsbeth Leibacher**. Born on 1 Jan 1670 in Nuerensdorf, Canton,

Zurich, Switzerland. Kunrad died in Nuerensdorf, Canton, Zurich, Switzerland, on 3 Jul 1729; he was 59.

On 7 Jul 1691 when Kunrad was 21, he married **Anna Egolf**[165] in Nuerensdorf, Zurich, Switzerland.

65. Anna Egolf.[165] Born on 28 Jul 1669 in Nuerensdorf, Zurich, Switzerland. Anna died in Nuerensdorf, Zurich, Switzerland, on 17 Jan 1722; she was 52.

66. Jakob Morff.

Jakob married **Regula Binder.**

67. Regula Binder.

100. Joseph Allen[166,167,168,169,170], son of **200. Joseph Allen**. Joseph died in Braintree, Norfolk, Massachusetts, on 16 Apr 1727; he was 55.[166,168] Born on 3 Jan 1672 in Braintree, Norfolk, Massachusetts.[166] Buried in Braintree, Norfolk County, Massachusetts, United States of America.[166]

On 14 Aug 1701 when Joseph was 29, he married **Abigaill Savell**[171,172] in Braintree, Suffolk.

101. Abigaill Savell.[171,172] Born on 14 Feb 1678 in Braintree, Norfolk, Massachusetts.[171] Abigaill died in Braintree, Norfolk, Massachusetts, on 8 Jan 1746; she was 67.[171] Buried in Braintree, Norfolk County, Massachusetts, United States of America.[171]

104. Johann Adam Roder[173,174,175,176,177,178], son of **208. Adam Diether Roder** & **209. Anna Uhrig**. Born in 1669 in Canton, Bern,

Switzerland.[175,176] Buried in Emmaus, Lehigh County, Pennsylvania, United States of America.[176] Johann Adam died in Mutterstadt, Ludwigshafen, Rheinland-Pfalz, Germany, on 23 Mar 1721; he was 52.

In 1700 when Johann Adam was 31, he married **Anna Katharina TAUBER**[179,180,181] in Mutterstadt, Ludwigshafen, Rheinland-Pfalz, Germany.[175]

105. Anna Katharina TAUBER.[179,180,181] Born on 12 Nov 1670 in Canton, Bern, Switzerland. Anna Katharina died in Emmaus, Lehigh, Pennsylvania, United States, on 19 Apr 1751; she was 80.

GENERATION 8

128. Jog li Ringger, son of **256. Heinrich Ringger** & **257. Usula Schwarz**. Born on 1 Jan 1642 in Nuerensdorf, Canton, Zurich, Switzerland.

25/10/1664 when Jog li was 22, he married **Elsbeth Leibacher**.

129. Elsbeth Leibacher. Born in Wangen.

200. Joseph Allen.[182] Born on 15 May 1650 in Braintree, Norfolk County, Massachusetts, United States of America.[182] Joseph died in Braintree, Norfolk County, Massachusetts, United States of America, on 20 Mar 1727; he was 76.[182] Buried in Braintree, Norfolk County, Massachusetts, United States of America.[182]

208. Adam Diether Roder[183,184,185,186], son of **416. Hans Röder** & **417. Elisabetha KOP.** Born on 8 Apr 1649 in Niedernhausen,

Darmstadt-Dieburg, Hesse, Germany. Adam Diether died in Brandau, Darmstadt-Dieburg, Hesse, Germany, on 2 Feb 1713; he was 63.

In 1677 when Adam Diether was 27, he married **Anna Uhrig**[187] in Neunkirchen, Darmstadt-Dieburg, Hessen, Germany.

209. Anna Uhrig.[187] Born on 17 May 1656 in Reichelsheim, Odenwaldkreis, Hessen, Germany. Anna died in Lengfeld, Darmstadt-Dieburg, Hessen, Germany, on 1 May 1696; she was 39.

GENERATION 9

256. Heinrich Ringger, son of **512. Hans Ringger** & **513. Anna Steffen**. Born 24/5/1611 in Nuerensdorf, Canton, Zurich, Switzerland.

On 5 Oct 1638 when Heinrich was 27, he married **Usula Schwarz** in Ruemlingen.

257. Usula Schwarz. Born in Ruemlingen.

416. Hans Röder.[188] Born in 1610 in Neunkirchen, Darmstadt-Dieburg, Hessen, Germany. Hans died in Hessen, Darmstadt, Hessen, Germany, in 1658; he was 48.

On 30 Nov 1635 when Hans was 25, he married **Elisabetha KOP**[189] in Dem Schloss Lichtenberg Bei Gross, Hessen, Germany.

417. Elisabetha KOP.[189] Born on 11 May 1617 in Niedernhausen. Elisabetha died in Niedernhausen on 10 Dec 1686; she was 69.

GENERATION 10

12. Hans Ringger[190], son of **1024. Kilian Ringger** & **1025. Verena Leibacher**. Born on 2 Apr 1572 in Nuerensdorf, Canton, Zurich, Switzerland.

Hans married **Anna Steffen**.

513. Anna Steffen.

GENERATION 11: 1024. Kilian Ringger[191], son of **2048. Hans Ringger** & **2049. Elsi Mueller**. Born on 10 Oct 1543 in Nuerensdorf, Canton, Zurich, Switzerland.[191] Kilian died in 1585; he was 41.[191] Buried in Zurich, Bezirk Zürich, Zürich, Switzerland.[191]

Kilian married **Verena Leibacher**.

1025. Verena Leibacher.

GENERATION 11

2048. Hans Ringger.[192] Hans died in 1581; he was 61.[192] Buried in Zurich, Bezirk Zürich, Zürich, Switzerland.[192] Born in 1520 in Nuerensdorf, Canton, Zurich, Switzerland.[192]

Hans married **Elsi Mueller**[193].

2049. Elsi Mueller.[193] Born in 1520.[193] Elsi died in 1571; she was 51.[193] Buried in Zurich, Bezirk Zürich, Zürich, Switzerland.[193]

Rinker Ancestral Lineage Sources

1   Date of Import: October 9, 1999

2   "1900 United States Federal Census," Ancestry.com, Ancestry.com Operations Inc, 1,7602::0, Ancestry.com, Year: 1900; Census Place: Kensett, Worth, Iowa; Roll: 468; Page: 10B; Enumeration District: 0149; FHL microfilm: 1240468.

     1,7602::16386416

3   "1910 United States Federal Census," Ancestry.com, Ancestry.com Operations Inc, 1,7884::0, Ancestry.com, Year: 1910; Census Place: Grove, Worth, Iowa; Roll: T624_429; Page: 4A; Enumeration District: 0172; FHL microfilm: 1374442.

     1,7884::7765072

4   "U.S., Find A Grave Index, 1600s-Current," Ancestry.com, Ancestry.com Operations, Inc., 1,60525::0, Ancestry.com.

     1,60525::48251758

5   "Iowa, State Census Collection, 1836-1925," Ancestry.com, Ancestry.com Operations Inc, 1,1084::0, Ancestry.com.

     1,1084::5910291

6   "1880 United States Federal Census," Ancestry.com and The Church of Jesus Christ of Latter-day Saints, Ancestry.com Operations Inc, 1,6742::0, Ancestry.com, Year: 1880; Census Place: Ashby, Shenandoah, Virginia; Roll: 1390; Family History Film: 1255390; Page: 489C; Enumeration District: 087.

     1,6742::19174325

7   "Web: Washington County, Maryland, Marriage Index, 1861-1949," Ancestry.com, Ancestry.com Operations, Inc., 1,70012::0, Ancestry.com.

     1,70012::158424

8   "Indiana, Marriages, 1810-2001," Ancestry.com, Ancestry.com Operations, Inc., 1,60282::0, Ancestry.com.

1,60282::4449460

9 "Ancestry Family Trees," Online publication - Provo, UT, USA: Ancestry. com. Original data: Family Tree files submitted by Ancestry members., Ancestry.com.

Ancestry Family Tree

http://trees.ancestry.com/pt/AMTCitationRedir.aspx?tid=77309604&pid=8387

10 "Iowa, Wills and Probate Records, 1758-1997," Ancestry.com, Ancestry.com Operations, Inc., 1,9064::0, Ancestry.com, Will Records, 1858-1956; Author: Worth County (Iowa). Clerk of the District Court; Probate Place: Worth, Iowa.

1,9064::1854916

11 "1870 United States Federal Census," Ancestry.com, Ancestry.com Operations, Inc., 1,7163::0, Ancestry.com, Year: 1870; Census Place: Ashby, Shenandoah, Virginia; Roll: M593_1678; Page: 641A; Image: 407062; Family History Library Film: 553177.

1,7163::36943927

12 "Iowa, Marriage Records, 1923-1937," Ancestry.com, Ancestry.com Operations, Inc., 1,8823::0, Ancestry.com, Iowa State Archives; Des Moines, Iowa; Volume: 389 (Dallas - Fremont).

1,8823::3588530

13 Date of Import: May 8, 2004

14 "1900 United States Federal Census," Ancestry.com, Ancestry.com Operations Inc, 1,7602::0, Ancestry.com, Year: 1900; Census Place: Kensett, Worth, Iowa; Roll: 468; Page: 10B; Enumeration District: 0149; FHL microfilm: 1240468.

1,7602::16386417

15 "1910 United States Federal Census," Ancestry.com, Ancestry.com Operations Inc, 1,7884::0, Ancestry.com, Year: 1910; Census Place: Grove, Worth, Iowa; Roll: T624_429; Page: 4A; Enumeration District: 0172; FHL microfilm: 1374442.

1,7884::132401093

16 "U.S., Find A Grave Index, 1600s-Current," Ancestry.com, Ancestry.com Operations, Inc., 1,60525::0, Ancestry.com.

1,60525::48252135

17 "1880 United States Federal Census," Ancestry.com and The Church of Jesus Christ of Latter-day Saints, Ancestry.com Operations Inc, 1,6742::0,

Ancestry.com, Year: 1880; Census Place: Springfield, Dane, Wisconsin; Roll: 1422; Family History Film: 1255422; Page: 344C; Enumeration District: 089. 1,6742::46089706

18 "1930 United States Federal Census," Ancestry.com, Ancestry.com Operations Inc, 1,6224::0, Ancestry.com, Year: 1930; Census Place: Saratoga, Howard, Iowa; Roll: 659; Page: 4B; Enumeration District: 0017; Image: 206.0; FHL microfilm: 2340394.
1,6224::27720245

19 "1920 United States Federal Census," Ancestry.com, Ancestry.com Operations Inc, 1,6061::0, Ancestry.com, Year: 1920; Census Place: Northwood, Worth, Iowa; Roll: T625_518; Page: 8A; Enumeration District: 185; Image: 990.
1,6061::44588445

20 "Iowa, Marriage Records, 1923-1937," Ancestry.com, Ancestry.com Operations, Inc., 1,8823::0, Ancestry.com, Iowa State Archives; Des Moines, Iowa; Volume: 389 (Dallas - Fremont).
1,8823::903588530

21 "Iowa, State Census Collection, 1836-1925," Ancestry.com, Ancestry.com Operations Inc, 1,1084::0, Ancestry.com.
1,1084::1537312

22 "Iowa, Marriage Records, 1923-1937," Ancestry.com, Ancestry.com Operations, Inc., 1,8823::0, Ancestry.com, Iowa State Archives; Des Moines, Iowa; Volume: 1.
1,8823::1203294250

23 "Ancestry Family Trees," Online publication - Provo, UT, USA: Ancestry. com. Original data: Family Tree files submitted by Ancestry members., Ancestry.com.
Ancestry Family Tree
http://trees.ancestry.com/pt/AMTCitationRedir.aspx?tid=77309604&pid=8386

24 Date of Import: Aug 16, 1999

25 "Iowa, Marriage Records, 1923-1937," Ancestry.com, Ancestry.com Operations, Inc., 1,8823::0, Ancestry.com, Iowa State Archives; Des Moines, Iowa; Volume: 389 (Dallas - Fremont).
1,8823::1053588530

26 "Rockingham County, Virginia Deaths, 1878-1885," Ancestry.com, Ancestry. com Operations Inc, 1,4588::0, Ancestry.com.
1,4588::1332

27 "U.S., Find A Grave Index, 1600s-Current," Ancestry.com, Ancestry.com Operations, Inc., 1,60525::0, Ancestry.com.
1,60525::24657673

28 "1850 United States Federal Census," Ancestry.com, Ancestry.com Operations, Inc., 1,8054::0, Ancestry.com, Year: 1850; Census Place: District 58, Shenandoah, Virginia; Roll: M432_976; Page: 99B; Image: 203.
1,8054::15541012

29 "1860 United States Federal Census," Ancestry.com, Ancestry.com Operations, Inc., 1,7667::0, Ancestry.com, Year: 1860; Census Place: Mount Clifton, Shenandoah, Virginia; Roll: M653_1377; Page: 645; Family History Library Film: 805377.
1,7667::34745861

30 "1880 United States Federal Census," Ancestry.com and The Church of Jesus Christ of Latter-day Saints, Ancestry.com Operations Inc, 1,6742::0, Ancestry.com, Year: 1880; Census Place: Ashby, Shenandoah, Virginia; Roll: 1390; Family History Film: 1255390; Page: 489C; Enumeration District: 087.
1,6742::42916070

31 "Virginia, Select Marriages, 1785-1940," Ancestry.com, Ancestry.com Operations, Inc, 1,60214::0, Ancestry.com.
1,60214::4725611

32 "1870 United States Federal Census," Ancestry.com, Ancestry.com Operations, Inc., 1,7163::0, Ancestry.com, Year: 1870; Census Place: Ashby, Shenandoah, Virginia; Roll: M593_1678; Page: 641A; Image: 407055; Family History Library Film: 553177.
1,7163::40383534

33 "Virginia, Compiled Marriages, 1851-1929," Ancestry.com, Ancestry.com Operations Inc, 1,4498::0, Ancestry.com.
1,4498::24620

34 "Virginia, Compiled Census and Census Substitutes Index, 1607-1890," Ancestry.com, Ancestry.com Operations Inc, 1,3578::0, Ancestry.com.
1,3578::33874651

35 "U.S., Civil War Soldier Records and Profiles, 1861-1865," Historical Data Systems, comp, Ancestry.com Operations Inc, 1,1555::0, Ancestry.com.
1,1555::2958099

36 "Ancestry Family Trees," Online publication - Provo, UT, USA: Ancestry. com. Original data: Family Tree files submitted by Ancestry members., Ancestry.com.
Ancestry Family Tree
http://trees.ancestry.com/pt/AMTCitationRedir.aspx?tid=77309604&pid=12269

37 "Iowa, Marriage Records, 1923-1937," Ancestry.com, Ancestry.com Operations, Inc., 1,8823::0, Ancestry.com, Iowa State Archives; Des Moines, Iowa; Volume: 389 (Dallas - Fremont).
1,8823::1203588530

38 "U.S., Find A Grave Index, 1600s-Current," Ancestry.com, Ancestry.com Operations, Inc., 1,60525::0, Ancestry.com.
1,60525::98504095

39 "1860 United States Federal Census," Ancestry.com, Ancestry.com Operations, Inc., 1,7667::0, Ancestry.com, Year: 1860; Census Place: Mount Clifton, Shenandoah, Virginia; Roll: M653_1377; Page: 645; Family History Library Film: 805377.
1,7667::34745862

40 "1880 United States Federal Census," Ancestry.com and The Church of Jesus Christ of Latter-day Saints, Ancestry.com Operations Inc, 1,6742::0, Ancestry.com, Year: 1880; Census Place: Ashby, Shenandoah, Virginia; Roll: 1390; Page: 489C; Enumeration District: 087.
1,6742::42915955

41 "Ancestry Family Trees," Online publication - Provo, UT, USA: Ancestry. com. Original data: Family Tree files submitted by Ancestry members., Ancestry.com.
Ancestry Family Tree
http://trees.ancestry.com/pt/AMTCitationRedir.aspx?tid=77309604&pid =12263

42 "1870 United States Federal Census," Ancestry.com, Ancestry.com Operations, Inc., 1,7163::0, Ancestry.com, Year: 1870; Census Place: Ashby, Shenandoah, Virginia; Roll: M593_1678; Page: 641A; Image: 407056; Family History Library Film: 553177.
1,7163::39377977

43 "1860 United States Federal Census," Ancestry.com, Ancestry.com Operations, Inc., 1,7667::0, Ancestry.com, Year: 1860; Census Place: Powels

Fort, Shenandoah, Virginia; Roll: M653_1377; Page: 746; Family History Library Film: 805377.
1,7667::34199937

44 "1850 United States Federal Census," Ancestry.com, Ancestry.com Operations, Inc., 1,8054::0, Ancestry.com, Year: 1850; Census Place: District 58, Shenandoah, Virginia; Roll: M432_976; Page: 138A; Image: 280.
1,8054::15544221

45 "1880 United States Federal Census," Ancestry.com and The Church of Jesus Christ of Latter-day Saints, Ancestry.com Operations Inc, 1,6742::0, Ancestry.com, Year: 1880; Census Place: Johnston, Shenandoah, Virginia; Roll: 1390; Family History Film: 1255390; Page: 414B; Enumeration District: 085.
1,6742::19171302

46 "1870 United States Federal Census," Ancestry.com, Ancestry.com Operations, Inc., 1,7163::0, Ancestry.com, Year: 1870; Census Place: Johnson, Shenandoah, Virginia; Roll: M593_1678; Page: 685A; Image: 410381; Family History Library Film: 553177.
1,7163::40384287

47 "U.S. Civil War Soldiers, 1861-1865," National Park Service, Ancestry.com Operations Inc, 1,1138::0, Ancestry.com.
1,1138::5181189

48 "American Civil War Soldiers," Historical Data Systems, comp., Ancestry.com Operations Inc, 1,3737::0, Ancestry.com, Side served: Confederacy; State served: Virginia.
1,3737::6026293

49 "Virginia, Select Marriages, 1785-1940," Ancestry.com, Ancestry.com Operations, Inc, 1,60214::0, Ancestry.com.
1,60214::4721800

50 "Virginia, Select Marriages, 1785-1940," Ancestry.com, Ancestry.com Operations, Inc, 1,60214::0, Ancestry.com.
1,60214::1624355

51 "1830 United States Federal Census," Ancestry.com, Ancestry.com Operations, Inc., 1,8058::0, Ancestry.com, 1830; Census Place: Western District, Shenandoah, Virginia; Series: M19; Roll: 200; Page: 139; Family History Library Film: 0029679.
1,8058::940909

52 "1820 United States Federal Census," Ancestry.com, Ancestry.com Operations, Inc., 1,7734::0, Ancestry.com, 1820 U S Census; Census Place: Mount Pleasant, Shenandoah, Virginia; Page: 146; NARA Roll: M33_138; Image: 160.

1,7734::1096023

53 "U.S. and International Marriage Records, 1560-1900," Yates Publishing, Ancestry.com Operations Inc, 1,7836::0, Ancestry.com, Source number: 488.000; Source type: Electronic Database; Number of Pages: 1; Submitter Code: BDJ.

1,7836::1023490

54 "Virginia, Compiled Marriages, 1740-1850," Ancestry.com, Ancestry.com Operations Inc, 1,3723::0, Ancestry.com.

1,3723::32398

55 "Family Data Collection - Individual Records," Edmund West, comp., Ancestry.com Operations Inc, 1,4725::0, Ancestry.com, Birth year: 1788; Birth city: Conicville; Birth state: VA.

1,4725::4655202

56 "U.S., Find A Grave Index, 1600s-Current," Ancestry.com, Ancestry.com Operations, Inc., 1,60525::0, Ancestry.com.

1,60525::77071674

57 "1840 United States Federal Census," Ancestry.com, Ancestry.com Operations, Inc., 1,8057::0, Ancestry.com, Year: 1840; Census Place: Shenandoah, Virginia; Roll: 578; Page: 356; Family History Library Film: 0029692.

1,8057::1936743

58 "Ancestry Family Trees," Online publication - Provo, UT, USA: Ancestry. com. Original data: Family Tree files submitted by Ancestry members., Ancestry.com.

Ancestry Family Tree

http://trees.ancestry.com/pt/AMTCitationRedir.aspx?tid=77309604&pid=14421

59 "Virginia, Select Marriages, 1785-1940," Ancestry.com, Ancestry.com Operations, Inc, 1,60214::0, Ancestry.com.

1,60214::1624356

60 "U.S. and International Marriage Records, 1560-1900," Yates Publishing, Ancestry.com Operations Inc, 1,7836::0, Ancestry.com, Source number:

488.000; Source type: Electronic Database; Number of Pages: 1; Submitter Code: BDJ.

1,7836::153386

61 "1840 United States Federal Census," Ancestry.com, Ancestry.com Operations, Inc., 1,8057::0, Ancestry.com, Year: 1840; Census Place: Shenandoah, Virginia; Roll: 578; Page: 355; Image: 728; Family History Library Film: 0029692.

1,8057::1936714

62 "Virginia, Compiled Marriages, 1740-1850," Ancestry.com, Ancestry.com Operations Inc, 1,3723::0, Ancestry.com.

1,3723::1032398

63 "U.S., Find A Grave Index, 1600s-Current," Ancestry.com, Ancestry.com Operations, Inc., 1,60525::0, Ancestry.com.

1,60525::98504069

64 "Virginia, Select Marriages, 1785-1940," Ancestry.com, Ancestry.com Operations, Inc, 1,60214::0, Ancestry.com.

1,60214::4721801

65 "Ancestry Family Trees," Online publication - Provo, UT, USA: Ancestry.com. Original data: Family Tree files submitted by Ancestry members., Ancestry.com.

Ancestry Family Tree

http://trees.ancestry.com/pt/AMTCitationRedir.aspx?tid=77309604&pid=14420

66 "Virginia, Compiled Marriages, 1740-1850," Ancestry.com, Ancestry.com Operations Inc, 1,3723::0, Ancestry.com.

1,3723::40373

67 "U.S., Find A Grave Index, 1600s-Current," Ancestry.com, Ancestry.com Operations, Inc., 1,60525::0, Ancestry.com.

1,60525::107767610

68 "U.S. Army, Register of Enlistments, 1798-1914," Ancestry.com, Ancestry.com Operations Inc, 1,1198::0, Ancestry.com.

1,1198::37945

69 "1830 United States Federal Census," Ancestry.com, Ancestry.com Operations, Inc., 1,8058::0, Ancestry.com, 1830; Census Place: Western District, Shenandoah, Virginia; Series: M19; Roll: 200; Page: 131; Family History Library Film: 0029679.

1,8058::940686

70 "1840 United States Federal Census," Ancestry.com, Ancestry.com Operations, Inc., 1,8057::0, Ancestry.com, Year: 1840; Census Place: Shenandoah, Virginia; Roll: 578; Page: 354; Family History Library Film: 0029692.

1,8057::1936676

71 "1820 United States Federal Census," Ancestry.com, Ancestry.com Operations, Inc., 1,7734::0, Ancestry.com, 1820 U S Census; Census Place: New Market, Shenandoah, Virginia; Page: 143; NARA Roll: M33_138; Image: 157.

1,7734::1095787

72 "Family Data Collection - Deaths," Edmund West, comp., Ancestry.com Operations Inc, 1,5771::0, Ancestry.com.

1,5771::1827872

73 "Ancestry Family Trees," Online publication - Provo, UT, USA: Ancestry. com. Original data: Family Tree files submitted by Ancestry members., Ancestry.com.

Ancestry Family Tree

http://trees.ancestry.com/pt/AMTCitationRedir.aspx?tid=77309604&pid=12266

74 "Virginia, Select Marriages, 1785-1940," Ancestry.com, Ancestry.com Operations, Inc, 1,60214::0, Ancestry.com.

1,60214::899509

75 "Virginia, Compiled Marriages, 1740-1850," Ancestry.com, Ancestry.com Operations Inc, 1,3723::0, Ancestry.com.

1,3723::1040373

76 "Virginia, Select Marriages, 1785-1940," Ancestry.com, Ancestry.com Operations, Inc, 1,60214::0, Ancestry.com.

1,60214::894755

77 "1850 U.S. Federal Census - Slave Schedules," Ancestry.com, Ancestry.com Operations Inc, 1,8055::0, Ancestry.com.

1,8055::2986671

78 "Ancestry Family Trees," Online publication - Provo, UT, USA: Ancestry. com. Original data: Family Tree files submitted by Ancestry members., Ancestry.com.

Ancestry Family Tree

http://trees.ancestry.com/pt/AMTCitationRedir.aspx?tid=77309604&pid=12265

79 "Shenandoah County Marriage Bonds, 1772-1850," Ancestry.com, Online publication - Provo, UT, USA: Ancestry.com Operations Inc, 2006.Original data - Ashby, Bernice M. Shenandoah County Marriage Bonds, 1772-1850. Baltimore, MD, USA: Genealogical Publishing Co., 1996.Original data: Ashby, Bernice M. Shenandoah County M, 1,49359::0, Ancestry.com. https://search.ancestry.com/cgi-bin/sse.dll?db=FLHG-ShenandoahCntyMar r&h=103758&ti=0&indiv=try&gss=pt
1,49359::103758

80 "U.S., Find A Grave Index, 1600s-Current," Ancestry.com, Ancestry.com Operations, Inc., 1,60525::0, Ancestry.com.
1,60525::107767958

81 "U.S., Sons of the American Revolution Membership Applications, 1889-1970," Ancestry.com, Ancestry.com Operations, Inc., 1,2204::0, Ancestry.com, Volume: 352.
1,2204::706839

82 "U.S., Find A Grave Index, 1600s-Current," Ancestry.com, Ancestry.com Operations, Inc., 1,60525::0, Ancestry.com.
1,60525::78800385

83 "U.S. and International Marriage Records, 1560-1900," Yates Publishing, Ancestry.com Operations Inc, 1,7836::0, Ancestry.com, Source number: 21369.008; Source type: Family group sheet, FGSE, listed as parents; Number of Pages: 1.
1,7836::1023508

84 "Virginia, Compiled Marriages, 1740-1850," Ancestry.com, Ancestry.com Operations Inc, 1,3723::0, Ancestry.com.
1,3723::54466

85 "1820 United States Federal Census," Ancestry.com, Ancestry.com Operations, Inc., 1,7734::0, Ancestry.com, 1820 U S Census; Census Place: New Market, Shenandoah, Virginia; Page: 143; NARA Roll: M33_138; Image: 157.
1,7734::1095823

86 "Family Data Collection - Individual Records," Edmund West, comp., Ancestry.com Operations Inc, 1,4725::0, Ancestry.com, Birth year: 1749; Birth city: Shenandoah Co; Birth state: VA.
1,4725::2161113

87 "Virginia, Compiled Census and Census Substitutes Index, 1607-1890," Ancestry.com, Ancestry.com Operations Inc, 1,3578::0, Ancestry.com.
1,3578::32814846

88 "Abstract of Graves of Revolutionary Patriots," Hatcher, Patricia Law, Ancestry.com Operations Inc, 1,4110::0, Ancestry.com, Abstract of Graves of Revolutionary Patriots; Volume: 3.
1,4110::42658

89 "Ancestry Family Trees," Online publication - Provo, UT, USA: Ancestry.com. Original data: Family Tree files submitted by Ancestry members., Ancestry.com. Ancestry Family Tree
http://trees.ancestry.com/pt/AMTCitationRedir.aspx?tid=77309604&pid=16473

90 "U.S., Sons of the American Revolution Membership Applications, 1889-1970," Ancestry.com, Ancestry.com Operations, Inc., 1,2204::0, Ancestry.com, Volume: 352.
1,2204::706840

91 "Virginia, Compiled Marriages, 1740-1850," Ancestry.com, Ancestry.com Operations Inc, 1,3723::0, Ancestry.com.
1,3723::1054466

92 "Family Data Collection - Individual Records," Edmund West, comp., Ancestry.com Operations Inc, 1,4725::0, Ancestry.com, Birth year: 1753; Birth city: Stover Township; Birth state: VA.
1,4725::4323172

93 "Family Data Collection - Births," Edmund West, comp., Ancestry.com Operations Inc, 1,5769::0, Ancestry.com.
1,5769::2521189

94 "U.S. and International Marriage Records, 1560-1900," Yates Publishing, Ancestry.com Operations Inc, 1,7836::0, Ancestry.com, Source number: 21369.008; Source type: Family group sheet, FGSE, listed as parents; Number of Pages: 1.
1,7836::678258

95 "U.S., Find A Grave Index, 1600s-Current," Ancestry.com, Ancestry.com Operations, Inc., 1,60525::0, Ancestry.com.
1,60525::45438354

96 "Ancestry Family Trees," Online publication - Provo, UT, USA: Ancestry.com. Original data: Family Tree files submitted by Ancestry members., Ancestry.com.

Ancestry Family Tree

http://trees.ancestry.com/pt/AMTCitationRedir.aspx?tid=77309604&pid=16472

97 "Virginia, Compiled Marriages, 1660-1800," Dodd, Jordan, Ancestry.com Operations Inc, 1,3002::0, Ancestry.com.

1,3002::37001

98 "1820 United States Federal Census," Ancestry.com, Ancestry.com Operations, Inc., 1,7734::0, Ancestry.com, 1820 U S Census; Census Place: Rockingham, Virginia; Page: 127; NARA Roll: M33_139; Image: 142.

1,7734::1103665

99 "1810 United States Federal Census," Ancestry.com, Ancestry.com Operations, Inc., 1,7613::0, Ancestry.com, Year: 1810; Census Place: New Haven, Rockingham, Virginia; Roll: 67; Page: 132; Image: 00176; Family History Library Film: 0181427.

1,7613::663467

100 "U.S., Find A Grave Index, 1600s-Current," Ancestry.com, Ancestry.com Operations, Inc., 1,60525::0, Ancestry.com.

1,60525::131800873

101 "Ancestry Family Trees," Online publication - Provo, UT, USA: Ancestry. com. Original data: Family Tree files submitted by Ancestry members., Ancestry.com.

Ancestry Family Tree

http://trees.ancestry.com/pt/AMTCitationRedir.aspx?tid=77309604&pid=16486

102 "U.S., Find A Grave Index, 1600s-Current," Ancestry.com, Ancestry.com Operations, Inc., 1,60525::0, Ancestry.com.

1,60525::131800918

103 "Virginia, Compiled Marriages, 1660-1800," Dodd, Jordan, Ancestry.com Operations Inc, 1,3002::0, Ancestry.com.

1,3002::137001

104 "Ancestry Family Trees," Online publication - Provo, UT, USA: Ancestry. com. Original data: Family Tree files submitted by Ancestry members., Ancestry.com.

Ancestry Family Tree

http://trees.ancestry.com/pt/AMTCitationRedir.aspx?tid=77309604&pid=16485

105 "1810 United States Federal Census," Ancestry.com, Ancestry.com Operations, Inc., 1,7613::0, Ancestry.com, Year: 1810; Census Place:

Shenandoah, Virginia; Roll: 71; Page: 20; Image: 00043; Family History Library Film: 0181431.

1,7613::827649

106 "Warwickshire, England, Church of England Baptisms, Marriages, and Burials, 1535-1812," Ancestry.com, Ancestry.com Operations, Inc., 1,2416::0, Ancestry.com, Warwickshire County Record Office; Warwick, England; Warwickshire Anglican Registers; Roll: PG 2974; Document Reference: DR(B) 3/3.

1,2416::3984482

107 "Ancestry Family Trees," Online publication - Provo, UT, USA: Ancestry.com. Original data: Family Tree files submitted by Ancestry members., Ancestry.com.

Ancestry Family Tree

http://trees.ancestry.com/pt/AMTCitationRedir.aspx?tid=77309604&pid=16455

108 "Ancestry Family Trees," Online publication - Provo, UT, USA: Ancestry.com. Original data: Family Tree files submitted by Ancestry members., Ancestry.com.

Ancestry Family Tree

http://trees.ancestry.com/pt/AMTCitationRedir.aspx?tid=77309604&pid=16454

109 "Virginia, Select Marriages, 1785-1940," Ancestry.com, Ancestry.com Operations, Inc, 1,60214::0, Ancestry.com.

1,60214::894754

110 "1880 United States Federal Census," Ancestry.com and The Church of Jesus Christ of Latter-day Saints, Ancestry.com Operations Inc, 1,6742::0, Ancestry.com, Year: 1880; Census Place: Lee, Shenandoah, Virginia; Roll: 1390; Family History Film: 1255390; Page: 515C; Enumeration District: 088.

1,6742::19175033

111 "1850 United States Federal Census," Ancestry.com, Ancestry.com Operations, Inc., 1,8054::0, Ancestry.com, Year: 1850; Census Place: District 58, Shenandoah, Virginia; Roll: M432_976; Page: 90A; Image: 184.

1,8054::15540214

112 "1820 United States Federal Census," Ancestry.com, Ancestry.com Operations, Inc., 1,7734::0, Ancestry.com, 1820 U S Census; Census Place: Shenandoah, Virginia; Page: 458; NARA Roll: M33_138; Image: 151.

1,7734::1095392

113 "Virginia, Compiled Marriages, 1660-1800," Dodd, Jordan, Ancestry.com Operations Inc, 1,3002::0, Ancestry.com.
1,3002::37776

114 "Ancestry Family Trees," Online publication - Provo, UT, USA: Ancestry.com. Original data: Family Tree files submitted by Ancestry members., Ancestry.com.
Ancestry Family Tree
http://trees.ancestry.com/pt/AMTCitationRedir.aspx?tid=77309604&pid=16499

115 "U.S. and International Marriage Records, 1560-1900," Yates Publishing, Ancestry.com Operations Inc, 1,7836::0, Ancestry.com, Source number: 8841.227; Source type: Family group sheet, FGSE, listed as parents; Number of Pages: 1.
1,7836::1023324

116 "Family Data Collection - Births," Edmund West, comp., Ancestry.com Operations Inc, 1,5769::0, Ancestry.com.
1,5769::3783476

117 "U.S., Find A Grave Index, 1600s-Current," Ancestry.com, Ancestry.com Operations, Inc., 1,60525::0, Ancestry.com.
1,60525::72086793

118 "Family Data Collection - Deaths," Edmund West, comp., Ancestry.com Operations Inc, 1,5771::0, Ancestry.com.
1,5771::2204594

119 "U.S., Find A Grave Index, 1600s-Current," Ancestry.com, Ancestry.com Operations, Inc., 1,60525::0, Ancestry.com.
1,60525::97831517

120 "Ancestry Family Trees," Online publication - Provo, UT, USA: Ancestry.com. Original data: Family Tree files submitted by Ancestry members., Ancestry.com.
Ancestry Family Tree
http://trees.ancestry.com/pt/AMTCitationRedir.aspx?tid=77309604&pid=16569

121 "Virginia Land, Marriage, and Probate Records, 1639-1850," Ancestry.com, Ancestry.com Operations Inc, 1,7832::0, Ancestry.com.
1,7832::87007

122 "England, Select Births and Christenings, 1538-1975," Ancestry.com, Ancestry.com Operations, Inc., 1,9841::0, Ancestry.com.
1,9841::4900777

123 "Virginia, Compiled Census and Census Substitutes Index, 1607-1890," Ancestry.com, Ancestry.com Operations Inc, 1,3578::0, Ancestry.com. 1,3578::32937926

124 "U.S., Revolutionary War Rolls, 1775-1783," Ancestry.com, Ancestry.com Operations, Inc., 1,4282::0, Ancestry.com. 1,4282::908547

125 "New York, Genealogical Records, 1675-1920," Ancestry.com, Ancestry. com Operations Inc, 1,7831::0, Ancestry.com, American Archives (Series), 1774-1777 - Excerpts; Author: Force, Peter; Publication Place: Washington, D.C.; Publisher: Peter Force; Page Number: 1529. 1,7831::482294

126 "Pennsylvania, Land Warrants, 1733-1987," Ancestry.com, Ancestry.com Operations, Inc., 1,2409::0, Ancestry.com. 1,2409::92301

127 "North America, Family Histories, 1500-2000," Ancestry.com, Ancestry. com Operations, Inc., 1,61157::0, Ancestry.com, Book Title: Genealogy and biographical notes of John Parker of Lexington and his descendants : showing his earlier ancestry in America from Dea. Thomas Parker of Reading, Mass., from 1635-1893. 1,61157::131885

128 "Virginia, Compiled Census and Census Substitutes Index, 1607-1890," Ancestry.com, Ancestry.com Operations Inc, 1,3578::0, Ancestry.com. 1,3578::33880809

129 "U.S., Craftperson Files, 1600-1995," Ancestry.com, Ancestry.com Operations, Inc., 1,9063::0, Ancestry.com. 1,9063::102853

130 "Maryland, Compiled Census and Census Substitutes Index, 1772-1890," Ancestry.com, Ancestry.com Operations Inc, 1,3552::0, Ancestry.com. 1,3552::11372496

131 "Maryland, Compiled Census and Census Substitutes Index, 1772-1890," Ancestry.com, Ancestry.com Operations Inc, 1,3552::0, Ancestry.com. 1,3552::11424449

132 "New Kent County, Virginia Land Tax Records, 1782," Smith, Paulette, Ancestry.com Operations Inc, 1,3689::0, Ancestry.com. 1,3689::220

133 "Warwickshire, England, Church of England Baptisms, Marriages, and Burials, 1535-1812," Ancestry.com, Ancestry.com Operations, Inc., 1,2416::0, Ancestry.com, Warwickshire County Record Office; Warwick, England; Warwickshire Anglican Registers; Roll: PG 2974; Document Reference: DR(B) 3/3.

1,2416::153984482

134 "U.S., Quaker Meeting Records, 1681-1935," Ancestry.com, Ancestry.com Operations, Inc., 1,2189::0, Ancestry.com, Swarthmore College; Swarthmore, Pennsylvania; Minutes, 1759-1776; Collection: Baltimore Yearly Meeting Minutes; Call Number: RG2/B/H671 1.2.

1,2189::1107430157

135 "Ancestry Family Trees," Online publication - Provo, UT, USA: Ancestry.com. Original data: Family Tree files submitted by Ancestry members., Ancestry.com.

Ancestry Family Tree

http://trees.ancestry.com/pt/AMTCitationRedir.aspx?tid=77309604&pid=16638

136 "North America, Family Histories, 1500-2000," Ancestry.com, Ancestry.com Operations, Inc., 1,61157::0, Ancestry.com, Book Title: Genealogy and biographical notes of John Parker of Lexington and his descendants: showing his earlier ancestry in America from Dea. Thomas Parker of Reading, Mass., from 1635-1893.

1,61157::131886

137 "Family Data Collection - Individual Records," Edmund West, comp., Ancestry.com Operations Inc, 1,4725::0, Ancestry.com, Birth year: 1720; Birth city: Cecil; Birth state: MD.

1,4725::3694522

138 "American Genealogical-Biographical Index (AGBI)," Godfrey Memorial Library, comp., Ancestry.com Operations Inc, 1,3599::0, Ancestry.com.

1,3599::69357

139 "Ancestry Family Trees," Online publication - Provo, UT, USA: Ancestry.com. Original data: Family Tree files submitted by Ancestry members., Ancestry.com.

Ancestry Family Tree

http://trees.ancestry.com/pt/AMTCitationRedir.aspx?tid=77309604&pid=16637

140 "Virginia Land, Marriage, and Probate Records, 1639-1850," Ancestry.com, Ancestry.com Operations Inc, 1,7832::0, Ancestry.com.

1,7832::98581

141 "Family Data Collection - Individual Records," Edmund West, comp., Ancestry.com Operations Inc, 1,4725::0, Ancestry.com, Birth year: 1743; Birth city: Northhampton; Birth state: PA.

1,4725::4621798

142 "1810 United States Federal Census," Ancestry.com, Ancestry.com Operations, Inc., 1,7613::0, Ancestry.com, Year: 1810; Census Place: Harrisonburg, Rockingham, Virginia; Roll: 67; Page: 145; Image: 00201; Family History Library Film: 0181427.

1,7613::664594

143 "1790 United States Federal Census," Ancestry.com, Ancestry.com Operations, Inc., 1,5058::0, Ancestry.com, Year: 1790; Census Place: Nazareth, Northampton, Pennsylvania; Series: M637; Roll: 8; Page: 272; Image: 460; Family History Library Film: 0568148.

1,5058::330675

144 "Family Data Collection - Births," Edmund West, comp., Ancestry.com Operations Inc, 1,5769::0, Ancestry.com.

1,5769::3655123

145 "Ancestry Family Trees," Online publication - Provo, UT, USA: Ancestry. com. Original data: Family Tree files submitted by Ancestry members., Ancestry.com.

Ancestry Family Tree

http://trees.ancestry.com/pt/AMTCitationRedir.aspx?tid=77309604&pid=16642

146 "Ancestry Family Trees," Online publication - Provo, UT, USA: Ancestry. com. Original data: Family Tree files submitted by Ancestry members., Ancestry.com.

Ancestry Family Tree

http://trees.ancestry.com/pt/AMTCitationRedir.aspx?tid=77309604&pid=16641

147 "U.S., Revolutionary War Rolls, 1775-1783," Ancestry.com, Ancestry.com Operations, Inc., 1,4282::0, Ancestry.com.

1,4282::324554

148 "U.S. and International Marriage Records, 1560-1900," Yates Publishing, Ancestry.com Operations Inc, 1,7836::0, Ancestry.com, Source number: 76.000; Source type: Electronic Database; Number of Pages: 1; Submitter Code: BDJ.

1,7836::1023323

149 "Virginia, Compiled Census and Census Substitutes Index, 1607-1890," Ancestry.com, Ancestry.com Operations Inc, 1,3578::0, Ancestry.com. 1,3578::33881648

150 "Pennsylvania, Compiled Census and Census Substitutes Index, 1772-1890," Ancestry.com, Ancestry.com Operations Inc, 1,3570::0, Ancestry.com. 1,3570::28165247

151 "Ancestry Family Trees," Online publication - Provo, UT, USA: Ancestry. com. Original data: Family Tree files submitted by Ancestry members., Ancestry.com.

Ancestry Family Tree

http://trees.ancestry.com/pt/AMTCitationRedir.aspx?tid=77309604&pid=16546

152 "Ancestry Family Trees," Online publication - Provo, UT, USA: Ancestry. com. Original data: Family Tree files submitted by Ancestry members., Ancestry.com.

Ancestry Family Tree

http://trees.ancestry.com/pt/AMTCitationRedir.aspx?tid=77309604&pid=16545

153 "England, Select Births and Christenings, 1538-1975," Ancestry.com, Ancestry.com Operations, Inc., 1,9841::0, Ancestry.com. 1,9841::4900778

154 "Ancestry Family Trees," Online publication - Provo, UT, USA: Ancestry. com. Original data: Family Tree files submitted by Ancestry members., Ancestry.com.

Ancestry Family Tree

http://trees.ancestry.com/pt/AMTCitationRedir.aspx?tid=77309604&pid=16725

155 "Ancestry Family Trees," Online publication - Provo, UT, USA: Ancestry. com. Original data: Family Tree files submitted by Ancestry members., Ancestry.com.

Ancestry Family Tree

http://trees.ancestry.com/pt/AMTCitationRedir.aspx?tid=77309604&pid=16724

156 "U.S. and Canada, Passenger and Immigration Lists Index, 1500s-1900s," Ancestry.com, Ancestry.com Operations, Inc, 1,7486::0, Ancestry.com, Place: Pennsylvania; Year: 1724-1725; Page Number: 284. 1,7486::3023565

157 "Family Data Collection - Births," Edmund West, comp., Ancestry.com Operations Inc, 1,5769::0, Ancestry.com. 1,5769::3655132

158 "Virginia Land, Marriage, and Probate Records, 1639-1850," Ancestry.com, Ancestry.com Operations Inc, 1,7832::0, Ancestry.com.

1,7832::98572

159 "Ancestry Family Trees," Online publication - Provo, UT, USA: Ancestry.com. Original data: Family Tree files submitted by Ancestry members., Ancestry.com.

Ancestry Family Tree

http://trees.ancestry.com/pt/AMTCitationRedir.aspx?tid=77309604&pid=17159

160 "Germany, Select Births and Baptisms, 1558-1898," Ancestry.com, Ancestry.com Operations, Inc., 1,9866::0, Ancestry.com.

1,9866::57664515

161 "U.S., Sons of the American Revolution Membership Applications, 1889-1970," Ancestry.com, Ancestry.com Operations, Inc., 1,2204::0, Ancestry.com.

1,2204::1013097

162 "U.S., Sons of the American Revolution Membership Applications, 1889-1970," Ancestry.com, Ancestry.com Operations, Inc., 1,2204::0, Ancestry.com.

1,2204::1013098

163 "Ancestry Family Trees," Online publication - Provo, UT, USA: Ancestry.com. Original data: Family Tree files submitted by Ancestry members., Ancestry.com.

Ancestry Family Tree

http://trees.ancestry.com/pt/AMTCitationRedir.aspx?tid=77309604&pid=17158

164 "Ancestry Family Trees," Online publication - Provo, UT, USA: Ancestry.com. Original data: Family Tree files submitted by Ancestry members., Ancestry.com.

Ancestry Family Tree

http://trees.ancestry.com/pt/AMTCitationRedir.aspx?tid=77309604&pid=16702

165 "Ancestry Family Trees," Online publication - Provo, UT, USA: Ancestry.com. Original data: Family Tree files submitted by Ancestry members., Ancestry.com.

Ancestry Family Tree

http://trees.ancestry.com/pt/AMTCitationRedir.aspx?tid=77309604&pid=16701

166 "U.S., Find A Grave Index, 1600s-Current," Ancestry.com, Ancestry.com Operations, Inc., 1,60525::0, Ancestry.com.

1,60525::17438249

167 "Bristol, England, Select Church of England Parish Registers, 1720-1933,"
Ancestry.com, Ancestry.com Operations, Inc., 1,9842::0, Ancestry.com.
1,9842::762521

168 "Massachusetts, Town and Vital Records, 1620-1988," Ancestry.com,
Ancestry.com Operations, Inc., 1,2495::0, Ancestry.com.
1,2495::82144614

169 "England & Wales, Christening Index, 1530-1980," Ancestry.com, Ancestry.
com Operations, Inc., 1,1351::0, Ancestry.com.
1,1351::4473529

170 "Ancestry Family Trees," Online publication - Provo, UT, USA: Ancestry.
com. Original data: Family Tree files submitted by Ancestry members.,
Ancestry.com.
Ancestry Family Tree
http://trees.ancestry.com/pt/AMTCitationRedir.aspx?tid=77309604&pid=17156

171 "U.S., Find A Grave Index, 1600s-Current," Ancestry.com, Ancestry.com
Operations, Inc., 1,60525::0, Ancestry.com.
1,60525::14805662

172 "Ancestry Family Trees," Online publication - Provo, UT, USA: Ancestry.
com. Original data: Family Tree files submitted by Ancestry members.,
Ancestry.com.
Ancestry Family Tree
http://trees.ancestry.com/pt/AMTCitationRedir.aspx?tid=77309604&pid=17154

173 "Germany, Select Births and Baptisms, 1558-1898," Ancestry.com, Ancestry.
com Operations, Inc., 1,9866::0, Ancestry.com.
1,9866::57664513

174 "Hesse, Germany, Marriages, 1849-1930," Ancestry.com, Ancestry.com
Operations, Inc., 1,61118::0, Ancestry.com, Hessisches Hauptstaatsarchiv;
Wiesbaden, Deutschland; Bestand: 925; Laufende Nummer: 2385.
1,61118::1351238221

175 "U.S. and International Marriage Records, 1560-1900," Yates Publishing,
Ancestry.com Operations Inc, 1,7836::0, Ancestry.com, Source number: 396.000;
Source type: Electronic Database; Number of Pages: 1; Submitter Code: HFH.
1,7836::989516

176 "U.S., Find A Grave Index, 1600s-Current," Ancestry.com, Ancestry.com
Operations, Inc., 1,60525::0, Ancestry.com.

1,60525::71216695

177 "Pennsylvania and New Jersey, Church and Town Records, 1708-1985," Ancestry.com, Ancestry.com Operations, Inc., 1,2451::0, Ancestry.com, Historical Society of Pennsylvania; Philadelphia, Pennsylvania; Historic Pennsylvania Church and Town Records; Reel: 562.
1,2451::18938822

178 "Ancestry Family Trees," Online publication - Provo, UT, USA: Ancestry. com. Original data: Family Tree files submitted by Ancestry members., Ancestry.com.
Ancestry Family Tree
http://trees.ancestry.com/pt/AMTCitationRedir.aspx?tid=77309604&pid=17161

179 "Germany, Lutheran Baptisms, Marriages, and Burials, 1500-1971," Ancestry. com, Ancestry.com Operations, Inc., 1,61229::0, Ancestry.com.
1,61229::300062484

180 "Germany, Select Births and Baptisms, 1558-1898," Ancestry.com, Ancestry. com Operations, Inc., 1,9866::0, Ancestry.com.
1,9866::57664511

181 "Ancestry Family Trees," Online publication - Provo, UT, USA: Ancestry.com. Original data: Family Tree files submitted by Ancestry members., Ancestry.com.
Ancestry Family Tree
http://trees.ancestry.com/pt/AMTCitationRedir.aspx?tid=77309604&pid=17160

182 "U.S., Find A Grave Index, 1600s-Current," Ancestry.com, Ancestry.com Operations, Inc., 1,60525::0, Ancestry.com.
1,60525::6209524

183 "Germany, Select Births and Baptisms, 1558-1898," Ancestry.com, Ancestry. com Operations, Inc., 1,9866::0, Ancestry.com.
1,9866::22462785

184 "Germany, Select Deaths and Burials, 1582-1958," Ancestry.com, Ancestry. com Operations, Inc., 1,9868::0, Ancestry.com.
1,9868::3443713

185 "Germany, Select Marriages, 1558-1929," Ancestry.com, Ancestry.com Operations, Inc., 1,9870::0, Ancestry.com.
1,9870::20447390

186 "Ancestry Family Trees," Online publication - Provo, UT, USA: Ancestry. com. Original data: Family Tree files submitted by Ancestry members., Ancestry.com.

Ancestry Family Tree

http://trees.ancestry.com/pt/AMTCitationRedir.aspx?tid=77309604&pid=17163

187 "Ancestry Family Trees," Online publication - Provo, UT, USA: Ancestry. com. Original data: Family Tree files submitted by Ancestry members., Ancestry.com.

Ancestry Family Tree

http://trees.ancestry.com/pt/AMTCitationRedir.aspx?tid=77309604&pid=17162

188 "Ancestry Family Trees," Online publication - Provo, UT, USA: Ancestry. com. Original data: Family Tree files submitted by Ancestry members., Ancestry.com.

Ancestry Family Tree

http://trees.ancestry.com/pt/AMTCitationRedir.aspx?tid=77309604&pid=17165

189 "Ancestry Family Trees," Online publication - Provo, UT, USA: Ancestry. com. Original data: Family Tree files submitted by Ancestry members., Ancestry.com.

Ancestry Family Tree

http://trees.ancestry.com/pt/AMTCitationRedir.aspx?tid=77309604&pid=17164

190 "Switzerland, Select Burials, 1613-1875," Ancestry.com, Ancestry.com Operations, Inc., 1,60172::0, Ancestry.com.

1,60172::161974

191 "Global, Find A Grave Index for Burials at Sea and other Select Burial Locations, 1300s-Current," Ancestry.com, Ancestry.com Operations, Inc., 1,60541::0, Ancestry.com.

1,60541::8760884

192 "Global, Find A Grave Index for Burials at Sea and other Select Burial Locations, 1300s-Current," Ancestry.com, Ancestry.com Operations, Inc., 1,60541::0, Ancestry.com.

1,60541::8760886

193 "Global, Find A Grave Index for Burials at Sea and other Select Burial Locations, 1300s-Current," Ancestry.com, Ancestry.com Operations, Inc., 1,60541::0, Ancestry.com.

1,60541::8760887

194 "The Rinkers of Virginia, Their Neighbors & Kin and the Shenandoah Valley"

By Daniel Warrick Burruss · 1993

Index

Printed in the United States
by Baker & Taylor Publisher Services